# TODAY
# I AM A MAN

## LARRY RODNESS

Savant Books
Honolulu, HI, USA
2009

Published in the USA by Savant Books and Publications
2630 Kapiolani Blvd #1601
Honolulu, HI 96826
http://www.savantbooksandpublications.com

Printed in the USA

Edited by Ryan Greendyk
Cover Design by Yegor Yatsik
Cover Photos by Jack Simon and Jupiter Images

Copyright 2009 Larry Rodness. All rights reserved. No part of this work may be reproduced without the prior written permission of the author.

ISBN: 0-9841175-2-0
EAN-13: 978-0-9841175-2-9

All names, characters, places and incidents are fictitious or used fictitiously. Any resemblance to actual persons, living or dead, and any places or events is purely coincidental.

# Dedication

| First Generation | Second Generation |
|---|---|
| Harold | Jodi |
| Kay | Adam |
| Steven | Jonathan |
| Michael | Erin |
| Cheryl | |

# Acknowledgement

To my Writer's Block members - Reva, Anne, Herb and Diane for their abundant criticism and unwavering support. Special thanks to my loving and patient wife, Jodi.

# Table of Contents

| | |
|---|---|
| Chapter 1–The Present | 1 |
| Chapter 2–1963 | 7 |
| Chapter 3–The Present | 17 |
| Chapter 4–1963 | 19 |
| Chapter 5–The Present | 25 |
| Chapter 6–1963 | 29 |
| Chapter 7–The Present | 35 |
| Chapter 8–1963 | 39 |
| Chapter 9 | 45 |
| Chapter 10–The Present | 55 |
| Chapter 11–1963 | 59 |
| Chapter 12 | 60 |
| Chapter 13–The Present | 69 |
| Chapter 14–1963 | 73 |
| Chapter 15–The Present | 79 |
| Chapter 16–1963 | 83 |
| Chapter 17 | 87 |
| Chapter 18–The Present | 97 |
| Chapter 19–1963 | 99 |
| Chapter 20 | 107 |
| Chapter 21 | 111 |
| Chapter 22 | 125 |
| Chapter 23 | 133 |
| Chapter 24 | 139 |
| Chapter 25 | 153 |
| Chapter 26 | 163 |

| | |
|---|---|
| CHAPTER 27 | 173 |
| CHAPTER 28 | 179 |
| CHAPTER 29 | 187 |
| CHAPTER 30 | 195 |
| CHAPTER 31 | 199 |
| CHAPTER 32 | 205 |
| CHAPTER 33 | 211 |
| CHAPTER 34 | 217 |
| CHAPTER 35 | 225 |
| CHAPTER 36 | 237 |
| CHAPTER 37 | 247 |
| CHAPTER 38–THE PRESENT | 257 |
| CHAPTER 39 | 261 |
| CHAPTER 40 | 265 |
| ABOUT THE AUTHOR | 273 |

Today I am a Man

# CHAPTER 1

## THE PRESENT

I'm not going to say it was a fair fight because it wasn't supposed to be. You use whatever advantage you have because you never go into a fight hoping to lose. Still, the odds seemed even: I was about one-hundred and sixty pounds to his one hundred and thirty, but he was taller–close to five-foot nine and I was only five-foot five. He had youth but I had experience. He was fifteen and I was fifty.

I waited for him on the sidewalk by the schoolyard, wondering if he would have his buddies with him. If so this could go either way: when kids get a whiff of blood, anything can happen. Not that that was going to change my mind. At 3:20 P.M., the school bell rang on schedule and my heart began to thump like the first time I took a drag from a cigarette, or unhooked a girl's bra, or stole something from the corner store.

## Today I am a Man

To calm my nerves, I went over my plan in my head one more time, envisioning the outcome before it happened. I even rehearsed what I was going to say, something brief and to the point just before I put him down to make sure he'd have something to think about afterwards.

There he was, coming out the main doors with his friends, some of whom had even been in my house. But today they were hanging with the wrong kid. Just as well, maybe they'd learn a lesson too.

*Close in on him right off. Watch his feet. First shot to the nose. Then when he goes down, put the boots to the motherfucker.* Advice that had been jangling around in my head since childhood. I moved in from the side using the surge of home-bound students to cover my approach. Just a few more steps . . .

"Todd Holloway? Do you know who I am?"

"Yeah," he answered, as if I barely mattered in his world. That would change in about two seconds. I cocked my right arm and drove my fist straight into his nose. I chose this spot for two reasons: first, to cause the most amount of pain, and second, because the first one to land a punch in a fight generally wins. Instinctively, the kid brought his hands up to stem the flow of blood gushing out of his nostrils, which left his mid section unprotected. That's when I buried my other fist deep into his gut, knocking the wind out of him and sending him to the ground in tears. Not such a big man now, are you? His legs thrashed out at me, more to keep me away than to do any damage. Then I turned to his buddies and stared each of them in the eye to show them I wasn't afraid. I heard one of them call me a "fuckin' bully," but instead of rushing me he knelt down to help his friend while another ran back into the school to report the assault. When I knew for sure that young Holloway wasn't getting back up to fight again and the others weren't in the mood for a swarming, I turned and walked home to dinner.

Two hours later I was having pasta and shrimp with my wife, Linda, and our three children, Daniel–fifteen, Jesse–twelve, and Amy–seven, who all took turns complaining about how much smarter they were than their teachers, when there was a knock on the door. I opened it to find two police officers.

"Steven Goldman?"

I nodded yes, at which point the first officer informed me that I was under arrest. I heard my wife gasp and the kitchen chairs scrape the floor as the family came running, in time to witness the second cop snap a pair of handcuffs on my wrists. "What the hell is going on here? What are you doing to my husband?" Linda demanded frantically.

And who could blame her? Nothing like this had ever happened to anyone in our comfortable little family before. I had never been arrested nor broken the law, so my wife had every reason to be freaking out. But instead of answering her questions, the first cop simply stated in a dispassionate and officious voice that I would be allowed one phone call after I was taken to the police station and booked. With that, they led me down the front steps of my home to their cruiser parked in the driveway, which made me a witness to the next scenario I had anticipated with regret. A visit from a police cruiser in this neighborhood was as strange as a visit from a flying saucer, and as such, it brought the nosy neighbors out to gawk. It wasn't me I felt bad for, but my family, who was going to have to face some strange looks and uncomfortable questions for the next while from people we had counted on as our friends for over twenty odd years.

As the police tucked me into the back seat, I thought I caught a whiff of something that if bottled probably would have been marketed under the name "Deep Shit." I distracted myself for a moment by imagining what the label on such a perfume bottle might look like, until one of the officers brought me back to the present.

"Do you understand these rights as I have explained them to you?"

That's when I caught the eye of my son, Daniel, who stared at me, looking pale as a ghost. "Yes," I replied.

There are markers along our paths, life-altering

moments where we must make a choice to take one road or the other. Looking back at my family standing there helpless and bewildered on the driveway, I knew that what I had done that day had not only changed the course of my life, but theirs as well. I also knew that I would have done it again given the same circumstances, which led me to wonder whether this was really just an awkward misstep, a stumble along a relatively smooth journey, or rather the fulfillment of my destiny? Had my up-to-now pleasant little drive down the road of life hit a speed bump, or was that bump actually a series of connecting cause-and-effect dots that had been put into play almost 40 years ago? If so, then everything from then until now had simply been a pause in the action awaiting the inevitable. The funny thing was, the ironic thing was, they called *me* a bully, which was the furthest thing from the truth. *I* was the kid the bullies bullied.

Today I am a Man

# CHAPTER 2

1963

When it comes to school, adults will tell you that all the important tests are in the classroom, but that's because they've forgotten. Ask any kid and he'll tell you that the risk of failure and disgrace is a lot worse out there on the playing field, especially when it comes to picking sides for football. That's because every kid knows that no matter how good he thinks he is, he's generally kidding himself, and the truth always comes out when the captains pick their team mates. The longer you stand there waiting to hear your name, the worse it feels. And the only thing worse than watching your friends get picked before you is the utter humiliation of being picked last. Well, that wasn't my problem on that sunny afternoon in the fall of 1963, because that day I was one of the captains, and I knew who all the best players were in the sixth grade, and I also knew that after I picked them, we'd have this game sewn up. All that was left was the toss, heads or tails.

"Heads," I called, and heads it was.

"Your choice, Sandy, you wanna kick or receive?"

"Kick!" I shouted, without actually knowing what the implication of the word meant. The meaning did come to me shortly after though in the form of a kick in the ass from Brian, one of the best players on my team.

"You wanna kick? There's your kick, asshole! Any idiot knows you receive if you win the toss! Ain't you ever played football before?"

The truth was, I hadn't played very much at all because, being smaller than the other guys, no one ever picked me for football or basketball or hockey or any of the team sports. In fact it was a mystery why they even chose me to be captain until I realized by the smirks on my friends' faces that part of the sport that day was in watching to see what I'd do when I was put in that position. I wasn't a captain, I wasn't even a player. I was the ball, I was what was being played and all the guys knew it. Standing there with stupid grins on their faces they waited to see what I would do next–would I come up with a smart-ass answer or kick Brian back and take him on? I didn't do either. I had a better plan, I walked off the field hoping that at least one of my buddies would stick up for me and call me back. Instead, they went on with the game without me. Maybe getting picked last was better; at least then you knew where you stood.

"What do you do when a bully comes at you?" asked my Father that night at dinner.

"You walk away," replied my Mother.

"Wrong," he countered. "You stand up to him because if you don't, he'll keep coming at you again and again. Pass the California melon, please."

Dinner was the only time of day when all six of us were together − me, my folks, my brother Paul (nine), Dustin (six), and my baby sister, Honey (two). That's when the arguments flew as fast as the food, and the winner was generally the one who yelled the loudest or kept the argument going until the other one gave up.

Meet my Mom. She wasn't a big woman, but she made up for it in the way small, yappy dogs get your attention sooner than the big ones. Now if you're thinking I'm comparing my mother to a bitch, you're reading me wrong, I mean no disrespect. In fact, I admire her for teaching me that being small doesn't mean you should be ignored. It was a lesson we all needed to learn because the fact is we got the runt gene from our father, whose brothers were all six feet tall or more. With four kids in the house, everybody needed to be heard and in the end, it wasn't height or weight that won the day, but the one who could out-shout or outlast the other.

The bully business Dad was talking about had nothing to do with my football game earlier that day (there was no way I was going to tell him about that). He was talking about how Kennedy stood up to Khrushchev and the whole Cold War thing. Even up here in Canada we knew all about it. Huddled under our desks during our monthly air raid drills, we'd whisper to each other how it would happen: first, the Russian planes would buzz by us overhead on their way to attack the United States. Then would come the huge atomic blast and the mushroom cloud, and one by one all the big American cities would be blown to smithereens. We'd be spared a direct hit, but we knew the worst was yet to come because any American survivors would be transformed into hideous radioactive mutants who would eventually make their way up to us from the south. At the same time, we'd have to fight off the Russians who would attack us from the north. It would be a tough fight, but being hearty Canadians, in the end we would win. Then, after we beat those dirty Reds and torched the mutant zombies, it would be our job to re-populate the world, and for that we'd need women, lots of women. That's really what all us twelve year olds were waiting for.

It wasn't our war, you know, but we shared a border

with the Americans, so it's not like we could just get up and walk away. Besides, they were our friends and neighbors, we knew everything about them: their president, John F. Kennedy, their movie stars–Marilyn Monroe, James Dean, Jerry Lewis, Frankie and Annette. And because we all looked and talked so much alike, we'd even lend them some of our stars every once in a while, guys like Lorne Greene and Wayne and Shuster. In fact, that's how we saw this whole Cold War thing, as one big Hollywood movie –good guys versus bad guys, Kennedy versus Khrushchev, Democracy versus Communism.

Anyway, what my father meant about bullies was that the Americans and Canadians were friends and when your friend gets into a fight, you have to stand with him side by side (although nobody stood with me on the football field earlier that day). As for the Cold War, it never actually went hot and unfortunately life went on without bombs, mutants, or us having to re-populate the world. Our only consolation was that we were on the winning side so we had bragging rights (not that you could find many Communists in Toronto, Canada to brag to). Still, it was a big moment in history, and as it turned out, an even bigger one in our family.

"Pass the California melon, please," Dad asked again. Somebody passed the melon while the rest of us wondered what was up with our father. He wasn't acting 'crazy' exactly, but he did sound a little off, like a guy on his way to having a mental breakdown.

My dad wasn't a big man, but he was rock solid from all the physical work he did at the butcher shop, lugging sides of beef from the freezer and cutting up the carcasses on the butcher block. I'd come by his store every once in a while after school and watch him with his cleaver and his knives. He'd been doing this since he was fifteen and there was no one better in the shop at cutting down a side of beef into steaks or slicing a chicken into quarters. Sometimes I'd find him out front serving the customers and telling his favorite joke:

"A woman comes into the shop one day and asks for a whole chicken, fresh. The butcher hands her the chicken for inspection. She looks it up and down, left and right, and then she spreads its legs to smell the bird from behind–for freshness. The butcher pipes up: "Lady, could *you* pass that test?"

Everybody in the place would laugh, but no one as much as my Dad. He loved kibbitzing with the customers and when he was in his store, he was the boss, the captain of his ship. Not at home, though. With all his skills with knives and cleavers, my Dad was no match for my Mom. Nope, at home, the chick ruled the roost. Mom was smaller, what people her age called "fine-boned," and in fact, when my folks got dressed up to go out to a movie she could look pretty damn good for a mom. But having to raise four children and running the house on her own from morning 'til night also made her one tough cookie. Even so, tonight was different. Tonight the bickering between them stopped before it even began.

"After dinner I'm going to the store," I announced.

"Me too," chimed in Paul.

Oh, no, he wasn't! I hated him following me everywhere I went. How was a kid supposed to grow up with his younger brother tagging along behind him all the time? My mother would try to convince me that it was Paul's way of looking up to me, but the truth was that his "looking up" was dragging me down.

"He's not coming and he's not following me!" I shouted.

"Can we please have one dinner without an argument for a change?" Mom pleaded.

"Sure," I cracked. "If you let me kill him tonight, then tomorrow night there'll be no arguments."

"Stop it, both of you," ordered Dad. "No arguments, no killing, just pass the California cucumbers, please!"

Now I was really worried. What was stranger: all the weird salad talk, or Mom and Dad being on the same side? Had Armageddon come and gone without me knowing it? Had we been blasted into the next world or worse, been sent to Purgatory like in one of those Twilight Zone episodes where you get locked up in a department store after hours and slowly come to realize that the night watchman is really God who is deciding whether he'll send you to Heaven or to Hell? Who was I kidding? Living in this house with these people *was* hell. Every 12-year-old lives in hell, waiting to escape his family, and my escape was just a few blocks down the street at the corner store after dinner! But for that to happen, I needed to get the parents on my side.

"Got my geography test back today, got a B,"

Dad smiled, "Speaking of geography, did you know that in California, the average temperature is sixty to seventy degrees all year long, and that people grow their own fruit and vegetables in their back yards?" I knew it, my father was going mental right in front of my eyes!

"Sandy got a B in Geography," announced Paul, "but he didn't tell you about the D he got in math. Did you, *Sandy?*"

My fist shot into his shoulder like an old reflex. "That's it, both of you! Any more of this and we're not going!" said Mom.

"Going? Going where?" I asked. My parents looked at each other and agreed that this was the moment.

"To California," announced Dad.

"As long as things down there are alright," my Mother added.

Talk about a bomb going off! A trip to California? We

never went anywhere, let alone to California. It's not like we were poor. We lived in a nice enough neighborhood, though you wouldn't call our house 'fancy.' The last vacation we took was to Crystal Beach on Lake Erie one summer, but that was only because my father got a job there as a butcher for the season.

"It's not a trip," Dad continued. "We're going to *live* in Los Angeles."

Talk about going mental! I was stunned, floored, dizzy as if my head was turning somersaults on my shoulders. I needed to get hold of myself and think this through: First, I'd be leaving all my relatives, but they could visit whenever they wanted to, so no big deal. Second, I'd be leaving my school and my friends, but after the way they treated me today, screw 'em. Besides, I'd make new friends, maybe even some famous ones. More importantly, I would be having my Bar Mitzvah in Los Angeles, California! Who could beat that? None of those assholes on the football field, that's for sure. My brother Paul cocked his skinny little head and squinted as if something didn't make sense.

"Would I still go to my same school?"

"Sure, we'll fly you back and forth every day so you can go to your stupid classes," I answered.

"Shut up, *Sandy*. Who asked you, *Sandy*? Mom, how come you gave *Sandy* a girl's name?" My fist flew out at him again, but this time my brother was half way down the hall before I could connect. I may have been older and stronger but he was faster. As I lurched out of my seat to finish off the little rat, my father said the magic words that probably saved him from certain death.

"You touch him, and we're not going!"

That's when it hit me, this was no joke. And as if to prove it, my father went on to explain how he hated the winters here and that it was always his dream to move somewhere warm like Los Angeles. What he didn't know was that this was my dream, too. It had been ever since I began taking guitar lessons at the local Y and learned all the latest Ricky Nelson songs. Now I was actually going to the land of Ricky Nelson and The Beach Boys! But even better than moving down to L.A. to give Ricky a run for his money, I realized that this was the solution to all my problems, my chance to leave all the bad stuff behind and start from scratch. No more getting picked last for football, no more getting picked on by the bigger guys. Pretty soon they'd be buying my records and begging me for my autograph! Only one more thing, and it would all be perfect.

"When we move, I'm changing my name. No more Sandy. From now on my name is Steve."

# CHAPTER 3

## THE PRESENT

I expected that the police might try to chat me up as they drove me to jail, perhaps even try to wring a confession out of me, but I found out later that they don't like to get involved because of all the extra paper work it generates. As it was, this incident was going to produce five to six hours of it between the two of them. What they would do is take notes on anything I said that might incriminate me, though I didn't offer much. Not that I didn't have a story to tell, but I wasn't going to take the chance on anyone misunderstanding my motives. I would tell them why I beat up young Todd Holloway in my way, on my own terms.

The cruiser arrived at the station fifteen minutes later

and pulled into an underground garage. Then the two officers helped me out of the cruiser and led me through a door called a Sally Port (something like an airlock with two sets of doors on either side) to a small booking room where their dreaded paperwork assignments began. From there, I was paraded in front of a Staff Sergeant.

"You can make one phone call to your wife or to your lawyer. If you don't have one, one will be appointed for you. Do you have any medical or physical complaints?"

"No," I answered.

"Are you suicidal?" For the first time that day I smiled.

"No."

# CHAPTER 4

1963

News about my move to L.A. changed my whole life just like I predicted. Overnight, I became a celebrity and instead of being picked on, I was picked first. Kids would point at me when I walked down the school corridors and whisper, "that's the kid who's going to L.A. That's the kid who's going to live with the movie stars."

Of course I had to dress the part, so I looked over the movie magazines "Tiger Beat," "Teen Beat," and all the other beats and got my mother to buy me what the cool guys like Ricky and Elvis and Brando wore. Dressed in a black shirt and black pants, with my jet black hair slicked down with Brylcream and my guitar slung across my chest, I was ready to be the next Teen Beat heart throb, although my father said I looked more like a hood than a movie star. But I didn't care because, instead of having to cross the gym floor to ask a girl to dance and getting rejected, the girls were crossing over and asking *me* to dance.

"So Sandy, when you get to Los Angeles, are you going to be a movie star?" they asked.

"I dunno, there're others ahead of me so I'll probably have to wait in line, but yeah, probably." The girls ate it up, but not the guys so much.

"Think you're hot stuff, doncha, just 'cause you're moving to L.A.?"

"No," came my humble reply, but 'yes' was written all over my face. Some of the guys called me conceited, which was the worst thing you could call a kid. This, of course, led to the inevitable shoving matches, but this was Canada and nobody here hardly ever threw a serious punch. In fact, I couldn't even remember seeing a bloody nose except maybe after one of our classic snowball fights. In the end, nothing those guys said mattered because I *was* hot stuff–hot from the glow of the golden California sun–and that was something no one here could take away from me. I had it all planned: finish public school at the end of the term and then disappear forever, leaving only the legend behind.

That was my plan, but I soon learned that the world of

the adult and the world of the kid moved as if they existed in separate solar systems. Adults were always planning for the future and hardly ever gave a thought to the moment. But for a kid, whether he was waiting to go to the store or waiting to go to the bathroom or waiting to go to Los Angeles, any delay could turn into an excruciating eternity. For me, every minute, every hour, and every day felt like painful drops from Chinese water torture machine while I suffered through another bone-crushing winter and rain-soaked spring until summer finally arrived, still without a firm moving date. And if the waiting wasn't enough, there was the worry of how pathetic I would be if I showed up at junior high school next fall with my friends waiting to tell me what a conceited, big-mouth, nobody I was.

      I got so depressed that my folks took pity and sent me off to Camp Lathaba, a day camp that specialized in Canadian Indian lore (and Canadian losers), about as far away from the glamour of Los Angeles as you could get. After two months of making head-bands and camp fires camp ended and we looked forward to our annual visit to the "Ex," (the Canadian National Exhibition), where for the price of admission you got to go on hundreds of rides. The best was the ferris wheel where the object of the ride was to eat enough cotton candy and hot dogs to throw up on the guy sitting below you. The C.N.E. signaled the end of summer and my humiliating return to school where I continued to build up resentment against my parents for failing to provide the exciting new life they had promised me. So I punished them by bringing home failing grades. I figured that if my life was going to disintegrate like Cool-Aid crystals in a glass of water, then someone was going to pay.

I can't say that everything was my parents' fault, although I wanted to. It was hard to blame them for the news that broke over the loudspeaker that November morning in French class: "We regret to interrupt your class with some very disturbing news. President John F. Kennedy has been shot in Dallas, Texas." Nobody said a thing, not even my teacher, Mrs. Abrams, until another teacher came in looking like she had been shot herself. The two of them held onto each other for dear life as if they'd mistakenly gotten onto one of those Tilt-A-Whirl rides at the "Ex." Here's a tip: if you ever want to scare the shit out of a kid, just put a couple of crying adults in the room.

He wasn't our president, but for us Canadians it felt like losing a favorite uncle. Even worse for me. A few days later, while we watched the funeral on T.V., it felt as if someone had come along with an ice cream scoop, hollowed out my insides, and then buried my dreams in JFK's coffin. Not my dad, though. That night he made a promise to the whole family.

"We're still going," was all he said, and he sounded so determined that nobody questioned him, not even Mom, and I loved him for that.

My birthday came and went that same month without the kind of fanfare a thirteen year old Jewish boy usually gets, because we were going to save my Bar Mitzvah celebration for after we moved to L.A.. Actually, I was glad my 'bar' was postponed because I saw how nervous my friends were when their time came. I don't know why; it's not like in Africa where they send you into the jungle to kill a lion and make you bring back its heart. Here, all a Jewish kid has to do is stand up, say a few prayers, and then go to this big party where the most dangerous part is when his uncles pick him up in a chair and try to toss him off again, while everyone dances the hora in a circle.

All the speeches sounded the same, and started off with "Today I am a man," and then the kid goes on to say what that means to him (or what their parents told him to say it means to him). If it was up to the kid himself, it would go something like, "Today I am a man in the eyes of my community. And what does being a man really mean to me? It means I can read Playboy magazines, buy cigarettes and beer, and watch any movie I want whenever I want. It means if I don't want to do my homework, I don't have to. If my parents want to ground me, I have the option of either ignoring them or telling *them* to go to *their* room. And when they ask why, I get to say 'because I said so.' I never heard that in anybody's

TODAY I AM A MAN

Bar Mitzvah speech. Maybe I'll use it in mine.

Anyway, a few months later, in February, Dad brought us all down to Union Station and put us on the train just like he promised. Aunts, uncles, and grandparents hugged us goodbye and sent us on our way with sloppy kisses, salty tears, and chocolates–in case we got hungry on the way. They all promised to come down for my Bar Mitzvah and I promised I would write them every week, but I would have promised anything including becoming a Rabbi if it meant having to spend one less minute in what felt like the coldest city in the world. Stepping onto the train and looking out through the frosted window as we left the station was the most exciting moment of my life. And it lasted until our first meal. Then the boredom set in. Three days of snowy landscapes, three days of never-ending fights with my kid brother Paul, who followed me for the entire three thousand miles up and down that damn train, until finally we opened the blinds on the fourth morning to see palm trees and feel the warm California sun. My dream had come true . . . but the nightmares were about to begin.

# CHAPTER 5

## THE PRESENT

    A half hour after being paraded in front of the staff sergeant, another officer escorted me into a small interview room devoid of furniture except for a metal chair that was cemented to the floor (in case I went on a rampage and tried to take out the entire police force). I waited there for over an hour until a detective finally entered. He seemed like a decent guy, and adopted a casual attitude as he introduced himself and ran down some background information on me, more or less to get a read on my current state of mind.

    "Are you comfortable? Do you need anything? Are you on any medication I should know about?"

    "No, I'm fine, thanks."

"Good. Would you like to tell me what happened?" When he realized that I was not going to answer, the detective paused to consult his notes before he continued, careful not to make any mistakes. I appreciated that about him.

"This young boy you assaulted, Todd Holloway, says he knows you, says he's friends with your son, Daniel. Says he's even been over to your house, is that right?" I nodded yes without explaining, so he nudged the conversation on a little further.

"Todd told me he came out of school after class today, that you came up to him, and without any provocation–which has been corroborated by a number of students who were there – punched him in the face and then in the stomach and waited for him to get up to do it again, is that accurate?"

"To be accurate, there was no provocation *today*. As for the fight, I punched him once in the nose and once in the stomach. I did wait for him to get up, but when I realized that he wasn't going to, I went home for dinner."

"So it sounds to me, Mr. Goldman, like this was something that had been brewing for a while, something you had been thinking about, something you planned. Would you like to tell me why you did it?"

"This is what you call my 'statement,' right? No thanks." Having researched police procedure before committing to my plan, I knew that "anything I said could be used against me,' just like you hear on those T.V. police shows. So it was in my best interest to say nothing to the detective and call my lawyer instead. However, the detective was good at his job and kept fishing, while studying me for any 'tell.'

"Does this have anything to do with drugs? Stolen goods? Money? Mr. Goldman, if you don't give me your statement, I will have to keep you here overnight in a cell."

"Not if my lawyer arranges bail," I countered.

"True, although it's already 8:00 o'clock and most lawyers are done for the day. Now, I can let you out myself on a Form 10 if I feel the circumstances warrant it. You don't have a record, or any priors, so chances are . . ." he said with promise in his voice.

"I think I'd like to call my lawyer now," I said firmly. The detective smiled and led me from the interview room back to the booking room, where I called my wife and asked her to call our lawyer. Knowing Linda, I knew she had gone to the phone the minute I was arrested, but my lawyer had told her that nothing could be done until morning. I assured her that I would be alright and there might even be a chance I'd be home tonight, even without his help. If not, I would see them both in court the next morning. Sitting a foot away, the detective could hear my wife's pleas through the phone for some kind of explanation for my irrational behavior. When he realized I wasn't going to give into her histrionics he made a gesture to terminate the conversation. I told Linda I loved her and would tell her everything when I saw her next. After I hung up the detective took a moment before he resumed his campaign.

"I'm sure she's very concerned for you right now, I know how women can get. Frankly, I don't blame her. Can I get you a drink? Are you ready to make your statement?"

"What if you don't like what I tell you?" I asked.

"It could work to your benefit, you know. Look, either way I have to make a report to the judge, which will include recommending bail or not, depending on what risk I think you might be to the public. As it stands now, I'd say that Todd Holloway is still at risk from you . . . unless you can tell me something that convinces me otherwise."

This was something I had not expected: how much sway this detective had on the outcome of my case. If I was stuck in jail, it would be more difficult for my wife and kids, who were the last ones I wanted to hurt. The stigma, my ability to earn money . . .

"Alright." He led me back to the interview room and took out his pen and notepad.

"So . . ."

# CHAPTER 6

1963

"Alfredo: Fail."

After a month or so of living in a tiny apartment in Van Nuys, we settled into a small bungalow in the lazy suburb of Canoga Park, tucked away in the San Fernando Valley. The worst part of it was having to share a bedroom with my brother, Paul. The best part of it, which outweighed all the other parts, was being able to run out into my backyard any time I wanted and look up at the mountains that surrounded us which made me feel like I was living in the greatest place in the world.

Like the mountains that circled the valley, a tall chain link fence circled Christopher Columbus Junior High School.

During classes, the corridors were patrolled by honor students whose job it was to report any students wandering around without a pass. After three days, I started to wonder if that fence was there to keep outsiders from getting in or to keep the students from getting at the innocent citizens who lived in the community.

Alfredo ambled up the aisle to get his paper with the slow, cool walk that Mexicans here all seemed to be born with. He had the added coolness of a kid who'd been held back a year. No one messed with Alfredo, not even Mrs. Clarke, our frumpy homeroom teacher.

"Joanne: C+." Joanne Metcalfe smiled to herself as she played with the hem of her dress.

"Beaver!" someone shouted as she got up to collect her paper. She had a sashay-kind-of-walk that showed off her brown, bouncy hair and cheerleader-type body that never spent a minute more on the athletic field than it had to. For this class, C was a good grade and Mrs. Clarke smiled as she handed over the paper. Joanne returned to her seat and stuck out her tongue at her boyfriend, Georgie Sparks, who's name was called next.

"Georgie: B."

"I don't believe it! What a browner!" came the catcalls, one louder than the other. Georgie, a blonde athletic surfer, puffed out his chest and strutted to the front of the room while the students challenged each other with more hoots and hollers until Mrs. Clarke clapped her hands for order, which was exactly what the kids were angling for because then they got to watch the fat dance under her arms, sending them all into hysterical fits of laughter. Then, while Mrs. Clarke's attention was elsewhere, it happened: When Georgie returned to his seat he tripped over Alfredo's foot–extended a little too far into the aisle. He whispered something under his breath to the Mexican and then faster than you could pull a switchblade, Alfredo was out of his seat with his fists clenched.

"No fights. No fights!" cried Mrs. Clarke. "Alfredo, do you want to see Mister Cole again?" Neither boy acknowledged her because down here, whoever flinched first was a chicken. Nothing interrupted the stare-down contest, not even the school bell when it rang. From experience, Mrs. Clarke knew that the room would explode if she didn't do something immediately.

"Everybody, on the whole, your grades are appalling and there's no reason for it. Now I want to see a change starting tomorrow or I will see to it that Mister Cole does some re-assigning." This was the second time Mrs. Clarke called upon the mysterious Mister Cole and it seemed to do the trick. The two boys broke off, grabbed their stuff and marched out of the room, which emptied as quickly as a twister ripping through Hurricane Alley. Mrs. Clarke heaved a sigh of relief until she noticed a couple of stragglers remaining. Maybe she felt sorry for me, the new kid, or was embarrassed about losing control of the room, or maybe this was her way of calming her own nerves, but she turned to me, and in her sweetest voice, said, "Steven, I'm expecting great things from you. Maybe one day you'll give us a talk about Canada."

"Sure, Mrs. Clarke, that would be fine." By the look on her face, I could see that this might have been the nicest conversation she'd had with any of her students all year and as a reward she called out to the other straggler, "Ricky, would you show Steven to his next class?" Ricky Mountjoy looked me up and down and grimaced at what he saw.

"Come on, greaser," he mumbled. When we got into the hallway, Ricky had already forgotten about me as he shuffled down the hallway. He was a head taller than me, with a slow, slouchy walk, like a guy trying real hard to be cool. Even with his lazy gait, he was a few bodies ahead of me, so I had to hurry to keep up.

"Uh, Ricky? Can you wait up? And just so you know, I'm not a greaser." He turned around to check me out in my black shirt, black pants, slick hair and smirked.

"So is that what surfers wear back where you come from? Fuckin' foreigners," he muttered, shaking his head pitifully.

"I'm not a foreigner, Ricky," I objected. "I'm

Canadian."

"And I'm not Ricky. Nobody calls me Ricky, okay? The name is Mounce." Before I could ask him what a Mounce was, I heard a thump down the corridor and we both turned to see Georgie pinned up against the lockers by Alfredo.

"You calling me a Beaner?" challenged the Mexican.

"You tripped me, asshole!" replied Georgie fearlessly.

As if some supersonic high-pitched signal had gone off, every kid from the four corners of the school showed up. They crowded around, jostling each other for the best position, waiting for the two to tear into each other, that was until Marguerita, Alfredo's big-haired girlfriend, whispered, "V.P. V.P.!"

Mounce craned his head over the mob to see Mister Cole, the Vice-Principal, approaching. This was the same man Mrs. Clarke had spoken about earlier, and just looking at him you could see the power that his name invoked. Dressed in a dark suit and tie, and armed with a dead-eye Dick look in his eye, he could as easily have been an army sergeant or a street cop as a middle school vice principle. Every student took two giant steps back as he marched up to the two boys.

"I've already seen you in my office once this month, Alfredo. You remember our discussion, don't you?" he said with a voice like a mix of gravel and steel.

"Swat," Mounce snickered. Mister Cole was not

someone to ignore and both boys broke off without another warning, but not before Alfredo whispered a challenge to Georgie. "I choose you off, man!" The edges of Georgie's lips curled into an icy smile as the two parted, Alfredo leading his gang of Mexicans down one corridor while Georgie and his friends swung down another.

"You can take him, Georgie."

"Wipe the floor with the slimy rape artist."

"We're all behind ya, man. It's gonna be bitchin'!" they shouted with encouragement. A bell rang and for a second I wasn't sure if I was at school or some boxing match.

Once everyone was out of hearing range, Mounce turned to me. "Georgie's gonna get his ass kicked. Look, don't talk to the beaners, don't cross the beaners, and whatever you do, don't call 'em beaners. The only thing worse than a beaner is Cole. Your next class is down that way. See ya at the fight, greaser."

Beavers, beaners, and greasers–there was so much to learn.

# CHAPTER 7

## THE PRESENT

The detective watched me with a patience gained from years of experience as I gathered my thoughts and sorted out the chronology of the events leading up to my assault on the fifteen year old student.

"My son Daniel and Todd Holloway have been friends for a year or so. Daniel was invited to a party at Todd's house last Friday night around seven-thirty. About an hour later, I got a call from Daniel asking me to pick him up, which I thought was a little odd. When I drove over, I found him standing on the street a few houses down from the party. As soon as he got into the car, I noticed that his face was bruised. He told me that he'd gotten into a fight with Todd. I asked him what it was about, but kids can be pretty vague when they want to be. All I got out of him was that he said something that Todd took the wrong way and got slugged for it. That's when my son left the party and called me. When I pressed him about the argument, Daniel said that everything would work itself out and that I should leave it up to him, which I did. I knew I was only hearing one side of the story, but my instinct was to let these kids handle it themselves. The following Monday, I got a call at work from my wife who said that Daniel had some trouble at school. The Holloway boy and his buddies had been pushing him around, you know–the kind of things kids do. I knew my son didn't have the experience to take on these kids himself, so I asked him if he wanted me to speak to Todd's parents. I got another no, and was told that he had friends at school who would protect him, and again he told me stay out of it. Next day, Tuesday, Daniel came home with a swollen eye. That's when I figured I'd better speak to Todd's parents."

"What happened when you went to the Holloway house?" asked the detective.

"His parents said they'd heard that Daniel was at their house the other night and said something 'out of turn,' some stupid thing about a girl, and that's why Todd asked him to leave."

"There was no mention of Daniel being beaten up?"

"No. Look, I know my son is no angel and he could

easily have said something. I just told Mister Holloway that I would make sure Daniel left Todd alone and asked the same from his son, to which he agreed. But next day, Daniel came home from school with more bruises. So this time, because it happened on school property, I went to the vice principal, Mrs. Drewry, and told her that Todd Holloway and his friends were bullying my son and that I wanted it to stop immediately. To her credit, she summoned Todd to the office and called him on it. Todd admitted that he might have been 'playing too rough' and that he would stop. I hoped that would be the end of it and in fact nothing happened for a couple of days until Daniel came home one night from the convenience store. Todd and his friends were there and kicked him around for 'ratting on them.' At that point, I was out of options."

"So you took the law into your own hands and beat up a fifteen year old kid?"

"I did what I had to do to protect my son. What would you have done?"

TODAY I AM A MAN

# CHAPTER 8

## 1963

    3:30 P.M. The school bell rang, the gates opened, and the students of Christopher Columbus spilled out into the sunny streets of the San Fernando Valley. A month ago, I was wearing a parka and snow boots; now I was wearing short sleeves and a sunburn. As I took a minute to close my eyes and thank God for this miracle, the grating sound of wheels against concrete roared up behind me. I turned around just in time to avoid Mounce colliding into me with his skateboard.

    "I choose you off, greaser!" he shouted playfully. Jogging next to him was Eddie Lopez, a wiry Mexican classmate of ours whose ever-present grin reminded me of a

Cheshire Cat.

"C'mon, we're going to the fight," said Mounce.

"Really think there'll be one?" I asked.

"Some guy chooses you off, you got no choice," stated Eddie. Mounce hung ten off his skateboard as he crossed the street and jumped the sidewalk.

"Probably be blades there too, huh, Eddie?" he shouted back.

"Blades? As in knives?"

"Sure, wadda they use in Canada, tomahawks?" Eddie replied in a snarky tone. The three of us followed the chattering crowd into the field and through the trees to a secluded meadow where everyone was clustering into groups – surfers, greasers, Mexicans, and nerds. I could see Georgie surrounded by his buddies, who were giving him last-minute instructions.

"Close in on him right off."

"Watch his feet."

"First shot to the nose. When he goes down, put the boots to the motherfucker."

The whole scene was like something on television, and it made me feel scared and excited at the same time. Mounce pushed his way into the surfer's huddle, full of teenage bravado.

"Wish it was me instead of you, man," he shouted.

Georgie looked at him as if to say, "Sure you do."

A few yards away, Alfredo received some last-minute advice from Marguerita and the other Mexicans. Pumped and primed, he turned to Georgie: "Hombre, you want it in the back or in the sack?"

The two boys strutted toward each other like gunslingers, the circle of students closing in behind them. They began taking turns, faking each other out with kicks and punches while each in the crowd shouted encouragement to his or her hero.

When Alfredo made first contact with a high kick to Georgie's arm it got real and the beaners hollered for blood. Georgie countered with a right hook, but Alfredo ducked and butted his head into Georgie's stomach. Georgie grabbed Alfredo around the gut in a bear hug and lifted him off his feet. Now it was the surfers' turn to howl. But as soon as Alfredo's feet touched ground he stomped on Georgie's foot. The Mexicans roared back.

Both boys locked arms and grappled like stags, testing each other's strengths and weaknesses. Georgie yanked Alfredo's arm, throwing him off balance and tripping him to the ground. Dirt and grass flew everywhere and then, in the blink of an eye, Georgie was on top of Alfredo's back, pounding his fist into his spine. They were slow, measured blows, almost as if Georgie was testing to see how deep the pain needed to go. "You give?" bellowed Georgie. Without getting an answer, Georgie drove another few into Alfredo with such resounding thumps that I could almost feel them myself.

"I don't believe it! Georgie's beating Alfredo!" Mounce screamed. "Get 'em, Georgie!"

Through all this Alfredo laid motionless in the dirt. It was hard to know if he was beaten, or trying to show how much punishment he could take, or was trying to gauge how strong Georgie was before he made his own move. In any case it didn't look good for Alfredo, and while the Mexicans stood there urging their hero get up and to fight back, it was Marguerita who took action, pulling a razor blade she'd hidden earlier out of her bee hive hair-do. Up until then, the fight had been kind of crazy and cool, like watching one of those wrestling matches everybody knows is fixed, but if she got that blade to Alfredo, real blood would flow.

Further back on the street, a purple muscle car pulled up and four big Mexicans got out. One of the surfer girls screamed a warning.

"Shit, it's Ricardo, Alfredo's brother!" whispered Mounce. Back home, somebody tripping somebody else might have led to a few choice words and maybe even a shoving match, but things were already looking as if they were going to turn into a blood bath, and if that happened, what the hell was I doing there? Everyone steeled themselves for a full-scale rumble. As if reading the fear in my eyes, Mounce whispered, "Stay behind somebody big."

Meanwhile, Marguerita inched closer to her boyfriend for the hand-off. The surfers warned her to get away but no one made a move towards her. Only Georgie seemed to defy this wildcat by staring her down, daring her to pass the blade to Alfredo. Why wouldn't any of the surfers take it out of her hand? Why didn't Georgie just climb off Alfredo to avoid getting stabbed? This was a wicked game of chicken nobody seemed to want stopped until Ricardo and his gang arrived and pulled Georgie off. I was new to all this, but even then I could guess what was going to happen next. Georgie sat there in the dirt and looked up at the hoods as if to say, "Go ahead, do your worst, I'll take it like a man."

Then a familiar gravel-edged voice called out. "Ricardo, back off! It's over." Mister Cole was on the scene and just like they did earlier today, the students stepped back to give him of room. Everyone except Ricardo, that is.

"This's public property an' I don't go to your school no more," Ricardo sneered.

Mr. Hunter, the big burly gym teacher, stepped up brandishing a baseball bat. "Ricardo, you remember me from a couple of years back?" he asked. Ricardo stared at both men for a long moment weighing the odds of him and his gang taking on these two husky men. The Mexican made his decision, picked up his younger brother, Alfredo, and led his gang out from the meadow and back to their car. Marguerita and the other Mexicans followed.

Mr. Cole looked at Georgie, barely concealing his pride. "You've had your fun. Now get out of here."

Georgie dusted himself off and strolled over to his girlfriend. Every surfer patted Georgie on the back as he passed them, as if hoping a little of his courage would rub off on them, too. "Bitchin' fight, man!"

"Knew you could take him!" offered Mounce, who jumped on my back. "I told ya. Didn't I tell ya? Surf rules!"

# CHAPTER 9

After the fight, Mounce walked me home and filled me in on what I needed to know if I was gonna make it here, like God giving Moses the ten commandments. One of the most important things, besides avoiding the beaners, was how to get around on a skateboard.

"This's hanging five, this is hanging ten, this is a one-eighty, this is a three-sixty, and this is a kick-flip, got it?" He demonstrated each of the tricks, watching me to make sure I was clear with each one of them, and then he put the board in my hands as if it were the sacred tablets. "Oak wood, laminated three times, ball-bearing wheels, best you can buy. You treat your board like it was your car, got it, man?"

By the time we got to his house, Mounce was huffing and puffing. He dropped onto his lawn which looked as smooth as a putting green on a golf course. The front door opened and Mounce's mom popped her head out. She was just like the lawn . . . or like one of those models who belonged on it with a golf club in one hand and a cocktail in the other. "Ricky, do you have your inhaler?"

Mounce nodded and pulled it out of his pocket as proof. "Don't wander off, dinner's within the hour," and then she disappeared back inside.

"Fuckin' asthma! Take off your shoes n' socks," he ordered. Mounce gestured for me to get on the skateboard as he continued his lecture. "The three most important things in life are your friends, your wheels, and your girl. Paying attention, greaser?"

"I told you, I'm not a greaser, Ricky."

"And I told you my name is Mounce. You don't call me Ricky, you don't call me Mountjoy. The name is Mounce, got it?"

He might not have believed me, but I did get it. The minute we decided to move to L.A., I stopped answering to 'Sandy.' My parents and friends could call me until their faces turned blue, but I wouldn't respond until they called me by my new name, Steven. So I knew how important it was for Mounce to go by his chosen name, but I also knew that if we were going to be friends, our relationship had to be based on mutual respect and equality and crap like that which meant that it wouldn't hurt for me to act a little tougher. "I'll call you Mounce if you call me Steven," I challenged.

"How's about if you call me Ricky again I pound you out?"

I nodded and he nodded, two tough guys coming to an agreement.

"So what are you–grease or surf?" he asked.

This question was harder and I didn't answer right away. I knew what he was really asking and I didn't want to make a mistake. A name is important, sure, but that is only part of who a guy is. The way he combed his hair and the style of his clothes determined where he ate lunch everyday and with whom he could hang out, which also determined what girls would date him and what his kids would look like when he got married. So for the sake of my unborn children, I didn't want to blow this.

"Look, I'm tryin' to help you out here man," Mounce continued. "I don't know how it is in Canada, but here you're either grease or surf. There ain't nothin' else, except those Honor nerds, and all they're good for is target practice." Hanging out with the Mexicans didn't seem like an option for me, even if they were taking Canadian members. Still, it didn't seem as black and white as Mounce made it out to be. Eddie Lopez was Mexican and he hung out with the surfers.

As if anticipating the question, Mounce answered,

## Today I am a Man

"Eddie's father plays for the California Angels, in case you're wondering - that makes him alright. His Mexican buddies will tell you he's a traitor, but the truth is, they'd do exactly the same thing if they got the chance. So, what are ya, surf or grease?"

Surf or grease? Black leather, bikes and hotrods, or blonde hair, shirt-tails, and surf boards? Neither felt like home to the Jewish boy from Canada. Elvis was grease, Marlon Brando was grease, even Ricky Nelson had greased-back hair. But on the other hand, I'd just seen a surfer beat up a greaser so maybe it was smart to pick friends closer to home.

What the hell; I climbed onto the skateboard suddenly realizing how easy it would be for me to roll down the sidewalk, into the street, and into the path of the cars whizzing by every three seconds. I turned the board around thinking it might be safer to head toward Mounce's garage, commending myself for being so smart, and thought how proud my Dad would be.

In fact, now that I was actually on the board, I was surprised at how good my balance was. If everything else proved as easy as this, I'd be one of the guys in no time. Betcha Elvis never even set foot on one of these things. Then, after I pushed off, I realized that I'd forgotten to ask Mounce how to stop. Lucky for me the garbage cans in the garage broke my fall.

"Jesus, man, what'd I just say about respecting your ride?" Mounce scolded me as he looked for any cuts or scrapes on his precious skateboard, but I didn't care. My eyes were fixed on a gleam coming from the corner of the garage, a gleam off what looked to be a set of cymbals and a snare drum.

"Whose are those?"

"Mine, whose do you think?" he barked, still checking out his board. Maybe I'd buy him a magnifying glass for his birthday, I thought.

"You play drums?"

"Ringo never took a lesson in his life. I've taken eight," Mounce boasted.

"I play guitar, been taking lessons for over a year," I boasted back.

"I have a band with my friend, Ronny Sheriff, he plays bass. You could try out for our group if you want."

"Bitching," I nodded.

"Bitchin'," he corrected me.

So the decision was made–I was officially surf. I mean, how could you have a greaser and a surfer in the same band? By the time I got home, I'd convinced myself that everything was coming together. It was fate, meant to be, "beshert" as they said in Hebrew. I mean if I hadn't met Mounce and we hadn't gone to the fight and then walked home together, I wouldn't have gotten on that skateboard and seen those drums, which meant I never would have joined a band that was destined to be bigger than The Beach Boys and tour the world and make a million dollars. Beshert!

As soon as I got to my bedroom, I whipped off the old black greaser duds and started training my hair to drop across one eye in that cool, surfer sweep. I caught my reflection in the bathroom mirror against the mountains behind our house and as far as I was concerned, I was the luckiest kid in the world. Surf ruled!

"It's been three weeks, Harold, and all our cash went into the down payment!" I heard my mother say. All the top-secret talks were held in my parents' bedroom next to my room because my folks figured no one could overhear them. But that was only true back home where the houses were made of concrete and plaster. Here, the homes were made of cheap plywood and you could hear just about everything through them.

"What are we going to do if you can't find work?" My mother loved to toss out questions like live hand grenades, ones that, if not handled just right, would explode in your face.

"Don't worry, I'll find work. Trust me, Fay, everything will be alright," was all my Dad could say. But this time he *was* right and with my newfound power I burst into their room to back him up.

"Dad, you were so right to bring us here. The

mountains, my new school–I've already made a new friend, and we're even starting a band. It's beshert!"

My parents looked at me with amusement.

"That's' not exactly what the word means," giggled my mother. "'Beshert' has more to do with the person you're destined to be with, the one you will love."

"You mean like you and Dad?"

My mother thought about it for a minute and then nodded, "Something like that."

"Well, then I'm right, because I'm in love with California. It's my 'beshert'!" I cried.

Before my mother could object or dampen my spirits with another of her grenades, the real bomb went off. Well, not a real bomb so much as an air raid siren. It was the sound we were taught to listen for back home: the one that sent us diving under our desks to protect us from radioactive fallout. The Russians had finally attacked! Everyone grabbed their most precious possession and hurried out onto the front lawn. My parents had Dustin and Honey, Paul was carrying his gold fish bowl, and I was holding onto my twelve dollar guitar for dear life. Frantically, we looked around to find where the nearest bomb shelter was and then noticed our next door neighbor, Mister Bowden, calmly tending his garden.

When he saw us he looked up and smiled. "They test the air raid sirens once a month, you know, ever since the

Cuban Missile Crisis."

My father broke out in a laugh, which only infuriated my mother who was carrying my shrieking baby sister under her arm back into the house. That's when I saw her for the first time—my next door neighbor, fifteen year-old Vicki Bowden, sitting on her door step, blonde, blue-eyed, dressed in a tank-top and cut-offs, the kind of California girl The Beach Boys sang about on their records – the gift, the prize, the reward. She looked at me standing on my lawn holding my guitar.

"Know any Beatles?" she asked, smiling sweetly.

"I don't know anybody in the neighborhood. We just moved here," I replied wondering what I had said that was so funny because she giggled and invited me over to her pool. My next door neighbor was a beautiful California blonde who had a pool!

"And bring your jams," she added.

Dad gave me a wink, code between two guys that meant thank you for helping with his woman, and that I had his okay to go after mine.

Fifteen minutes later, I was in Vicki's backyard holding a plate of bread with peanut butter and jam, and staring at the beautiful mermaid swimming the length of her pool.

"We only have grape jelly," I called out.

She stopped at the edge of the pool and giggled again.

"In L.A., jams means bathing suit. So who do you play? All the bands around here play the Ventures or the Beach Boys, but if you wanna be unique, I'd copy the Beatles. They're new and from England," she added with a smile as warm as the California sun. I watched Vicki climb out onto the deck, droplets of water dripping from her pastel bikini down her slim legs. She told me she was an actress and had just finished a Pepsodent commercial. Now she was up for a part in a T.V. series, something called Dobie Gillis. As Vicki went on about show business, I couldn't help wonder whether it was the water running down her bare legs or if it was her that made the water drops look so sexy. In fact everything, including my peanut butter and jelly sandwich, seemed just plain sexy that moment. "If you're serious about your music you should get an agent," she said, tossing the water from her long hair. Maybe one day I would, but at that moment I was too busy planning our wedding in this beautiful backyard garden, our parents at our sides, the Rabbi standing in front of us. Her voice seemed far off and yet barely a breath away at the same time. I heard her say that I'm already playing guitar, I might as well learn to sing, too, and answered, "I do." Then my brother, Paul, wrapped a glass in a napkin and placed it at my feet.

Before I could smash it and kiss my bride, her father called out, "Vicky, we'll be late for church."

TODAY I AM A MAN

# CHAPTER 10

## THE PRESENT

The detective took copious notes as we sat together in the interview room and I gave my statement. There was no heated lamp over my brow and no two-way mirror where other cops watched the interrogation. My objective was to tell my side of the story and convince him to release me. His objective was to write down the facts that led up to the incident for his report. Easy enough.

I described how I left the office of my small marketing firm at around two-thirty that afternoon, drove the approximately three miles to the neighborhood school, and parked across the street at the corner store.

Then I sat in my car listening to the radio for another fifteen minutes, waiting for classes to end. The detective interrupted me every once in a while to ask me to repeat a portion of my story as he referred back to his notes, I suppose, to try to catch me in a lie. But I wasn't here to lie, or to hide, or deny what I'd done, or even to make excuses for it. I was here to tell the truth. The trouble was, I was too honest.

"When we first brought you in, I looked you up on our database. You have no record," noted the detective.

"I know."

"So tell me, if I let you go tonight, what would you do?"

"I would go home."

"What would happen to Todd Holloway?"

"Nothing, as long as he left my son alone."

"In other words, if you went home and your son told you that this boy, Todd, hurt him again or said something to him, you'd go after the boy?"

That's when I realized the detective had a secret second agenda—while I was busy concentrating on the details of my story, he was trying to get a read on whether I was still a danger to the victim. If they released me and I went back to finish the job on Todd, the police would be in serious trouble.

"Mister Goldman. If your son told you that Todd hurt him again, would you go after the Todd?"

Sniffing a trap, I didn't answer. Unfortunately, the silence spoke for me.

"Based on that, I think you'll be staying with us overnight," he pronounced.

The police escorted me to a single cell about eight foot square with toilet and bed, and then confiscated my belt, shoelaces, and anything I could use to harm myself.

The detective went on to explain, "There are cameras everywhere so you don't want to be doing anything that might harm your case, understand?" Which was code for, "Please don't try to kill yourself on my watch, as it would mean even more paper work." I reassured him that I was in a healthy frame of mind, and as a reward for my cooperation he added, "I noticed you didn't have a chance to finish your dinner when we picked you up. Hungry?"

Fifteen minutes later, he brought me a plate of warmed over mashed potatoes and a ham sandwich with milk. Good thing I'm not an Orthodox Jew or he might've had a suicide on his hands right then and there.

## Today I am a Man

# CHAPTER 11

1963

The day finally came for me to give my talk to the class about Canada and I was pretty confident. I was always good in geography, so this was my chance to show off. "Canada is the second largest country in the world, second only to Russia. The United States in comparison is third."

And as soon as my ears heard what my brain informed my mouth to say, I knew I was in trouble. Americans didn't like coming in second to anything, and they certainly didn't like coming in third when it had anything to do with Khrushchev and his Commies. Every face in the room stared at me like I was a traitor and I got the feeling that if they could have lined me up against a wall and shot me, they would have.

"Eddie, how many states do we have?"

"Fifty-two, Mrs. Clarke," he replied smugly.

I got a sinking feeling in the pit of my stomach as I tried to defend myself. "We have ten provinces," I shot back, "*But* we have four seasons and our summers are just as warm as yours." This only got a big laugh from the class. As far as they were concerned, it snowed all year in Canada. They were wrong, of course, but now I was fighting for my life and I had to tell them something, anything, to convince them that I was not just some dick from Hicksville. "We have beaches, too–on our lakes." I was hoping to score some points at least with the surfers.

"Yeah, so when's the last time you surfed on a lake?" shouted John, the class clown, which pretty well shut me up. Then they started on about all the Indians living in Canada and me having relations with the Eskimo wives of my neighbors whenever I visited them. I told them I'd never even seen an Eskimo, let alone had relations with any Eskimo wife, but they kept going on and on until all I could think about was how I got in the position of defending the country I left, when all I wanted was to be part of the one I was in now. By the end of the talk, all I had succeeded in doing was showing them how different I was from them. Mrs. Clarke thanked me for the talk, but I really think she was thanking me for giving her class a chance to show off at my expense.

Mounce was the only one who gave me any encouragement, if you could call it that. "You shoulda talked more about the Eskimo broads, man. They were lappin' that shit up."

As we headed down the corridor to our next class, I noticed Georgie enter the bathroom, followed quickly by Alfredo and a couple of his Mexican pals. I told Mounce to wait for me, that I had to go to the bathroom, too. "It's called the head, stupid," he said. "And maybe you better hold it." Then he bent down and fiddled with his shoelace.

"I can't wait anymore," I told him as I walked into "the head." Funny how one stupid decision can change your whole life.

The sound of someone getting beaten is something unmistakable, even if you've never heard it before. As soon as I entered the head, my gut tightened and I got that fight or flight response they talked about in health class. Frozen with fear, I wondered whether should I say something or just run like hell. "V.P.! V.P.!" I shouted.

The pounding stopped and a minute later, Alfredo and his buddies, Manuello, and Carlos came out from behind the back stall. They looked me up and down and with their eyes, gave me a silent warning to keep my mouth shut or I'd get the same. After they left, I followed the hacking sounds around the corner to find Georgie on the ground holding his gut, blood smeared below him all over the tiles. My thoughts raced back to the fight in the field the other day and the razor blade Marguerita tried to hand to Alfredo. I crouched down beside him, fearing the worst. "Georgie, you okay?"

He pulled himself up and nodded his bloody head. Thank God, all the blood was from a single cut over his eyebrow. "Help me to the sink. I gotta wash off before Cole gets here."

"It's alright," I replied. "He's not coming. I just said he was." A smile crept over Georgie's face as he washed off. Then the door opened; it was Mounce.

"Jesus, Georgie, what happened? You get jumped by Alfredo and his punks?"

Georgie eyed Mounce suspiciously in the reflection of the mirror. "How'd you know that?" he asked.

Mounce coughed nervously and flipped his bangs over his eyes. "Uh, 'cause I just saw them comin' out, so I figured . . . damn, we'll get Turner and Blakeley and kick the shit out of those bastards." Mounce hacked even harder and pulled out his inhaler. Georgie finished cleaning up and punched me in the arm as he left – a sign of respect. Mounce got no such punch. He got ignored. "Come on, stupid," Mounce mumbled as he ambled out behind Georgie.

# CHAPTER 12

There was a short cut through the field most of us took when walking home after school and Mounce led me through it, whining all the way. "You know, you come down from that frozen wasteland of yours and we let you live here, and then all you do is yammer about how good it is back home. If it's so fuckin' good, why don't you go back where you came from?"

I tried to explain that the talk about Canada wasn't my idea, it was Mrs. Clarke's, but it made no difference. Then I got it; Mounce wasn't talking about class! What he was so pissed about was what happened back in the head and how Georgie reacted. I was just his closest target—until *we* became a target. Alfredo and his two friends were waiting for us up ahead behind a clump of trees. If we turned and ran, they'd be on us like a pack of wolves. If we kept walking . . . Hell, I wasn't born here, but even I knew we're gonna need a miracle to get us out of this one.

"Hey, Steve!" Georgie, Eddie Lopez, and four other surfers jogged up behind us. Thank you, God! "I didn't know you walked home this way. So do we. What a coincidence," Georgie said, more to Alfredo than to me as he led us right past the Mexicans who knew better than to start a fight when they were out-numbered. The only one who got an elbow in the ribs was Eddie, from one of his own, as he passed by the hostiles. When we were a safe distance away, I got the feeling that this was all part of a game in which everybody kept score for the next time. Then I got the feeling that even though I'd traveled over five thousand miles, I hadn't left my problems behind.

We dropped Mounce off at his house and as we continued on, the story about Georgie's attack and my quick thinking was told and retold so many ways that by the time I'd gotten home with my new friends, we were all so jazzed that we were ready to go to war with the beaners the next time they showed their ugly faces.

"So this is where ya live? Cool. Got a backyard?" asked Georgie.

"Sure," I replied, wondering why he would be so interested.

As we headed into the back, Vicki and her father drove up. She got out and waved at me as she trotted up to her front door, pretending not to notice the guys, who pretended not to notice her.

I had no idea what was so special about my backyard until Georgie looked it over then made straight for the bamboo thicket in the corner by the fence. Maybe he'd seen the tall stalks from the front of the house. Anyway, the guys pushed the bamboo aside, trampled the ground, and a minute later we had our own private fort. Neat, until Georgie lit up a cigarette and passed it around, which was when I understood why he wanted to see my backyard. Eventually, the butt got passed to me. I'd never smoked in my life but both my parents did, so I figured, why not? I took a polite puff.

"What is that?" bellowed Eddie. "You trying out for the girls' smoking team? Jesus, take a drag and swallow."

I inhaled, I coughed, they laughed. Talk shifted from the Mexicans to Vicki, who finished Christopher Columbus the year before. A few crude jokes were made, but I kept my mouth shut because getting in with these guys was way too important to jeopardize over some girl. Georgie started blowing smoke rings and a minute later everybody was doing it. I had to admit, it looked so cool. Of course, when I tried everyone laughed until Georgie gave them a look and they shut up.

"So, Steve, we're going out tonight. Wanna come?" he asked.

Wow, my quick thinking in the head earlier today had worked some serious magic. I really *must* be one of the guys. "Sure, but not too late 'cause of school tomorrow," I answered back.

"Midnight," announced Eddie, whose grin grew as quickly as mine vanished. "What are you chicken?"

Before I could reply, the patio door opened and my Dad called out. The cigarette was hastily put out and the blue air cleared before we left our fortress of solitude. Georgie led the way around the bamboo and was the first to introduce himself to my Dad. "Hi, I'm Georgie Sparks and these are the guys. We all go to school with Steven."

"Hi Georgie, nice to meet you," my father replied. "What are you all doing back there?"

"Oh, we thought we saw a fox or something. There are a lot of foxes around here," replied Eddie with a not-so subtle nod in Vicki's direction. My new friends made their excuses about dinner being ready and homework waiting.

"Your new friends, are they nice kids?" Dad asked suspiciously.

I noticed he was holding something behind his back which gave me an excuse to quickly change the subject.

"Yeah, sure. What's that you got?"

With a twinkle in his eye he brought his hand around to show me a little bush. "Remember that night back in

Toronto when I told you that if we moved here we could grow our own fruit? Well, this is our first pomegranate tree and I'm planting it to celebrate my new job."

"You got a job? Wow, great, Dad, I knew you would!" I watched him take a pen knife from his pocket and dig a hole next to the bamboo thicket. If he smelled cigarette smoke, he never said. He shoveled the loose dirt away and planted the little shrub in the hole he'd made while he talked about his new job at a butcher shop in downtown L.A. As I helped him clear the dirt it came to me that the tree was a symbol that he was putting down roots here. It was a little good-luck ceremony, a ritual just between me and my father, and it made me feel good sharing it with him. It also brought up another ritual.

"I promised you we'd get here, didn't I? I made a commitment to you and the family and now you have a commitment to your mother and me to study for your Bar Mitzvah—and we are expecting a perfect job."

"It will be, I promise," I said and I meant it.

Dustin and Paul came running out with a soccer ball and asked Dad if he wanted to play. He told them he was tired and asked me to take his place as he walked back into the house. Dad wasn't much of a sports guy and I was sure he was anxious to tell Mom about his new job. But when he tossed me the ball, I felt like this, too, was a ritual, making me the new man of the house, putting me in charge of the kids. This was a good moment, and when I thought back about everything that happened that today with Georgie and the guys and my father, I knew that everything was going to work out exactly the way I dreamed it would.

# CHAPTER 13

## THE PRESENT

At 6:00 A.M. the next morning, a Police Officer woke me up and passed me a plate of bacon, toast, and coffee. I had had a surprisingly good night's sleep, and felt that the worst was behind me. I mean, the detective seemed quite sympathetic, and after the judge heard my side of the story, how could he believe otherwise? I used the toilet in my cell and then ate breakfast, after which I was escorted in handcuffs through the sally port to the police parking lot.

I was put into a paddy wagon with several other prisoners and driven to the local courthouse. No one spoke, I suspect, for fear of compromising their position by giving anything away to the guards.

The twenty minute drive gave me some time to go over all the legal, moral, and psychological aspects of my argument I was about to present, not to the judge, but to my wife. The judge was trained to use logic and reasoning when determining culpability in such cases, and after I presented my side of the story, I was convinced that he would understand that I really had no other choice but to do what I had done. My wife, on the other hand, was not bound by such rules. When we arrived at the courthouse, I was led to an interview room where Linda and my lawyer were waiting. I had gone over my argument in my head, tied up every loophole, and was now prepared to face my fiercest interrogator to date.

"Are you crazy?" she screamed. "Beating up a fifteen year old boy?"

"I am not crazy. I had no other choice."

"There are always other choices besides violence," Linda replied vehemently. She liked to use those patented homilies that were logical, socially responsible, and impossible to argue. "Sure you were angry, but a mature person doesn't go around beating people up to solve his problems. Have you even thought about the repercussions, how it looked when the police drove you away in front of all of our neighbors, how it looked to your own children, how this might even affect your job? Do you realize we might have to move after all this is over, if it is ever over? What is wrong with you?"

Apparently, I was not the only person who had prepared for this meeting.

When my lawyer, married himself, recognized the obvious signs of a drowning man, he waded in to rescue me. "The important thing now is to get Steve home. Linda, can you get your hands on five thousand dollars if you have to?" The thought of having to bail her husband out of jail like a common thief shocked her into accepting the shift in the focus of the conversation.

As my lawyer figuratively swam me back to safety he continued: "Here's how it will go: I will propose bail and this being Steven's first offense, the judge will probably agree with certain stipulations. But right now, I need to talk with Steven alone to prepare him for court. The rest you can work out when he gets home. Can you please see about the money?"

As far as I was concerned my lawyer earned his fees right then and there. My wife pulled herself together and stood up. "Do those things hurt?" she said softly, referring to the handcuffs.

"No, I'm alright. You go; I'll see you soon. Love you." As she turned and left the room, I started to second-guess my original plan and the position in which I'd put my wife and kids. After getting a taste of her anger, I wondered whether jail might be the lesser of the two evils. Fortunately, I had little time to dwell on that because my lawyer needed me to run through my story, including anything I might have said to the arresting officers. Twenty minutes later, a cop approached and escorted me into court while my lawyer flashed me an emphatic thumbs up.

# CHAPTER 14

1963

Georgie called after dinner and briefed me on how to sneak out of the house late at night without getting caught. He said that it would be easy because no one would be expecting it. But he didn't have a little brother sleeping in the same room who would rat on him the first chance he got, so I had to improvise.

When it was time for bed, I sat up with a book and a flashlight to help me keep awake (as if I could sleep anyway). Paul had never seen me do that before, but I told him it was studying for a test and after a while he nodded off. When the clock closed in on twelve, I stuffed two pillows under my sheets, put on my robe, and went to the bathroom like I had to pee—in case anybody caught me in the hallway—which was part of Georgie's advice. When I got inside, I took my jeans, shirt and shoes out of the cupboard where I had stashed them earlier and put my bathrobe inside. Then I opened the window and climbed out. Easy as pie, just like Georgie had said.

The first thing I noticed outside was that the air at night was different than in the daytime. It was warm and sweet. If you could taste it, it would taste like something forbidden, like beer or liquor or maybe what it's like to be with a girl. Excited, I jogged to the front of my house and waited until I spotted two red dots in the dark distance coming toward me. As the dots got closer, they turned into cigarette butts and the cigarette butts into Georgie and Eddie. I didn't see Mounce with them, and wondered if maybe he was sick or couldn't get out or something. As the three of us headed down the street, the neighborhood felt spooky and dangerous and wonderful all at the same time; it felt like *anything* could happen.

I had a ton of questions to ask like, how long were we going to be out, where exactly were we going, and what was Georgie carrying in the bag? Still, I also wanted to be cool, and being cool meant not asking a lot of stupid questions. I figured I'd find out soon enough anyway. After we hiked a few blocks, we stopped at a street corner, where Eddie nudged Georgie. "That one? That one?"

Nope, Georgie had his eye on *that* one, a house with

the big tree in the front yard. They raced across the street and stared up at the tree. Then Georgie reached into his bag and pulled out a roll of toilet paper.

"What's that for?" My first stupid question.

Georgie took one end of the paper, whipped the roll up into the tree, and watched it wrap itself around a branch before dropped gently back to the ground. Eddie took another roll and lobbed it over the roof. Then he handed a third one to me. "What's wrong, ain't you ever T.P'd a house?" he asked.

"They can't do this up in Canada," Georgie proclaimed. "The paper's the same color as the igloos. Who'd notice?" Big laugh. We began tossing the rolls in different and imaginative ways until the exercise became a kind of toilet paper ballet.

"Who lives here?" My second stupid question.

"Who cares," answered Georgie. Then it was his turn to ask questions, but these weren't so stupid. "So the other day, outside the head at school, was Mounce with you or not?"

Now I knew why Mounce wasn't here. He wasn't invited because Georgie wanted to ask me about this without him around. What would be better, to lie and risk losing my new friendship with Georgie and Eddie, or tell the truth and risk losing Mounce's? I figured the best thing to do was act cool and say nothing, so I threw another roll over a branch. It seemed to work. After we'd finished decorating the entire property with toilet paper, we took a step back to admire our work: it looked like fucking Christmas in the middle of summer! I checked my watch and realized that we'd been out about an hour, and I started to worry about how I was going to wake up for school the next morning. That was when Eddie said, "Honors go to the new kid."

Honors? What the hell did that mean? It didn't take long to find out as Eddie pulled a match from his pocket and lit one of the paper strands dangling from the tree. Then Georgie asked again, "So Steve, the other day in the bathroom when Alfredo and his goons jumped me, you came in to help, but not Mounce, right? He was with you outside, but he didn't come in, right?"

I couldn't answer him now even if I wanted to. My attention was on the flames that were slowly creeping up the strands of paper. "Georgie, you oughta put that out," I told him. "This is no joke. We could start a fire." But Eddie must have thought it *was* a joke because he lit another strand and then another, and then the both of them left me there staring while they raced down the street. "Guys? Guys!" I pleaded, standing there like a jerk.

Georgie and Eddie were now a block away, watching to see what I'd do. Would I run away too, or would I try to stop the tree from catching fire? I called them for help again, beginning to feel desperate, but the only answer I got was laughter. Maybe I shouldn't have been so cool or maybe I should have told Georgie what he wanted to know, but there was no time to think about that now. I grabbed the closest flaming strands and pulled them down off the tree, but there were more well beyond my reach. Panicking, I climbed the tree and reached for the burning papers, some of which hung from limbs too far out for me to reach them. Another trail of paper ignited and then another. I could either jump and run or . . . fuck it, I pulled myself along the narrow branch and managed to rip off several more of the burning pieces, which floated harmlessly to the ground. As I reached for the last flaming ream, the branch I was on gave way and I dropped like a rock. The next thing I knew I was on the ground, looking up, and gasping for air. Feeling a sense of doom, I turned on my side to catch my breath and found the toilet paper I reached for smoldering in the grass beside me. Somewhere in the distance I think I heard applause.

"Better move it before the dude comes out to see how you trashed his house," called Georgie.

I was so pumped with fear, excitement, and adrenaline that all I could do was to get back up and hustle down the street with them to where the three of us had met, then race back home. The faster we ran, the harder we laughed until I worried that if we laughed any harder we might puke our lungs out on the sidewalk, but we didn't cut our stride until we got back to my house.

"Wait 'til the morning dew sets in," said Georgie. "The guy'll have a shit-fit tryin' to take the paper off." Another round of laughter, and then he said to me, "I know Mounce was with you yesterday and I know he chickened out. It's okay, you were right not to rat on him. Surf rules. See ya tomorrow." The guys lit up as they swaggered down the block, shrinking into two tiny red dots, and disappeared into the night.

I ran around the side of my house and climbed back in through the bathroom window. Once inside, I listened for any movement in the hallway. It was all clear, so I put my bathrobe back on over my clothes and tip-toed back into my bedroom to find my brother still asleep. Safe under the covers, I slipped off my clothes, stuffed them under my bed and thought to myself, *this was just about the greatest night of my life!* Next morning, I rushed through breakfast, hurried down the block and sure as shit, there was the homeowner cursing a blue streak as he picked wet toilet paper off his property. And you know what, I wasn't even tired!

# CHAPTER 15

## THE PRESENT

"This hearing is not about arguing the assault charges against you, Mr. Goldman. We are here today to discuss only the question of bail," pronounced the judge. As courtrooms go, this one was small with few officials. There was a judge in his fifties who presided over the court and a stenographer who sat below him. I sat off to the side in a wooden booth with Plexiglas windows, presumably built for the protection of the accused, me. To the right of my booth sat a police officer whose job it was to escort prisoners in and out of the courtroom and keep a watch on things. This was the same cop who had escorted me from the paddy wagon to the interview room and then into the courtroom.

Once he placed me in the booth he took off my handcuffs and I thanked him, imagining that he had done me this service because I was such a model prisoner and nice guy, but most likely he was just following procedure. Down in front of the judge sat my lawyer and adjacent to him, a female prosecutor. In the pews sat my wife, Linda, and Todd Holloway's parents, playing the part of the tortured victims to the hilt. Also in attendance were a few regulars who came to court as part of their daily entertainment.

The judge began reading the statement written by the Staff Sergeant regarding how serious a threat I might be to young Todd Holloway if I was let out on bail, and then invited my lawyer to respond. My lawyer argued that my threat to go after Todd if he bothered my son Daniel again, was voiced just after I was arrested, that I was upset, and that upon further reflection I promised not to contact or go near Todd if I was released. The prosecutor argued against letting me out at all, claiming that I was hot-headed and ruled by emotion, which might override reason at any moment. My lawyer argued back that I had no prior offenses and any actions I allegedly committed were prompted by a plan which was devised through reason rather than emotion, and based on that, the prosecutor's argument held no water. After some stern looks, the judge recommended twenty-five hundred dollars bail and a court order that I not come within 500 yards of Todd

Holloway, along with the surety of my wife. "Do you know, Mrs. Goldman, what a surety is, and the responsibilities that go along with it?" he asked.

Linda stood up and for the first time in her life, addressed a court, responding exactly as our lawyer had coached her, trying not to show any of the anxiety that I knew was racking every fiber of her being. "Yes, your honor, your worship. Besides posting bail, it will be my responsibility to make sure that my husband obeys whatever the court orders, which includes no contact with the victim."

"The victim *and* his family," the judge corrected. Linda nodded and turned her head just enough to catch the self-satisfied smiles on the Holloway's faces. The judge pronounced that I would be released once bail was posted, and that I'd have to return to the police station the following week to be fingerprinted and have a mug shot taken. Upon hearing this my wife lowered her head in shame. A court date to hear the actual assault charges was set for thirty days away. Then the judge asked me to stand up and questioned whether I understood all the conditions. "Yes, your Worship."

He concluded the hearing, at which point the Officer once again handcuffed his model prisoner and led me out of the courtroom. On the way out, I looked at Linda, offering her a thank-you smile and a silent promise that all would be well. And it would. All I had to do now was mind my own business.

TODAY I AM A MAN

# CHAPTER 16

1963

I still couldn't get over eating lunch in the sunshine every day. Back in Toronto, I'd have been stuck in a gloomy gym, the only thing I'd have to look forward to at the end of the day would be battling my way home through a snowstorm. But here I was, relaxing in an outdoor school cafe, getting a tan and having lunch with my buddies. Life couldn't be any better! I couldn't wait to tell Georgie and Eddie how everything turned out this morning, but as I made my way over to their table, I was hijacked by Alfredo, Manuello, and Carlos. "I, uh, already got a seat over there," I said.

"What's wrong with this one?" said Alfredo with a

bright smile.

Georgie and the surfers watched curiously as I was forced over to the Mexican table. If the beaners decided to jump me, I hoped to God my friends would save me before I got slaughtered. In the meantime, I had no choice but to take a seat and try to act normal − I mean, cool.

"Whatchu lookin' for?" asked Manuello.

"Vinegar for my French fries,"

"French fries? You mean chips," Lupe corrected me. "Why you want vinegar for your chips? My mother uses that shit to wash the floors, man. Waddya want that shit on your chips for?"

That was funny because I was thinking, why would anyone use perfectly good vinegar on floors when it was made to put on French fries? Foreigners. I looked around the table again.

"Now what?" asked Manuello again.

"A straw for my milk."

"Fuckin' foreigners, man. You're in L.A. now," he said as he ripped my milk carton open with his hands.

"I am not a foreigner," and to prove it I gulped down my milk straight from the carton, which only made everyone laugh. Apparently drinking milk from a carton did not make you an American or a tough guy.

Alfredo leveled his dark Mexican eyes at me, and with

a dead-serious look, said how it was. "You're a foreigner jus' like me. Your parents bring you here from another country, jus' like me. You see the nice homes, the clean streets, the pretty girls in their pretty dresses, an' you want it all, jus' like me. Your skin ain't so brown and your hair ain't so black, but you're still a foreigner jus' like me. And jus' like me, they're not gonna let you have any of it."

"This is America. Everybody has the same rights here," I answered defiantly.

"The only right you got," he replied, "is the right to fight." To prove his point, he punched me in the arm, hard enough to make me wince. "Ooh, Canada, you're gonna need to toughen up. Here, have some more milk."

One thing I had learned was not to show weakness. I got up with my food tray like it was no big deal and shoved off. When I got to the surfer's table, Georgie slid over and made room for me. I hoped what he and the others saw was me *not* running away from the Mexicans, not being afraid . . . but being cool. Georgie gave me a nod and the others at the table smiled. If I wasn't 'surf' before, I was now, all of us united against a common enemy.

Today I am a Man

# CHAPTER 17

"Joanne: B. Much better," Mrs. Clarke announced in a colorful tone. Joanne sauntered to the front of the class where Mrs. Clarke handed over her paper along with . . . what was that, a chocolate bar? Was I seeing things? One by one, as students were called, each one picked up their paper along with a chocolate bar! Was this how it was supposed to be, getting a sweetener for doing your homework? Because if it was, those lousy teachers back in Canada must have been hoarding all the school chocolate for themselves!

"She's protecting her job," Mounce whispered. "If we fail, it proves what a lousy teacher she is." Mounce's name was called next and he strutted to the front of the class for his reward. When he returned he shoved the bar down his pants and wriggled his pelvis at Susan Cathcart before taking his seat. "I ain't passin' another test 'til Clarke starts handing out cash," he said. "So what did Alfredo say to you at lunch?"

Mounce was sitting at the end of the lunch table today, farthest away from Georgie. I wasn't sure if it was because there was nowhere else to sit or because he was sent there, but I could see he wasn't happy about it, or the fact that Georgie made room for me to sit next to him. I didn't want to have to end up telling Mounce about last night and make him feel worse about not being invited on the run. At the same time, I was feeling pretty good about being accepted as one of Georgie's friends and I didn't want to rock the boat.

I wasn't sure how to answer Mounce. It was all getting so complicated. Thankfully, Alfredo's name was called next and the class was distracted when it was announced that he got a B. Some of the Mexicans boo-ed him good-naturedly until he walked up to Mrs. Clarke and put his hand out for his chocolate bar, "This is your second time through, Alfredo. You shouldn't need any extra encouragement."

Alfredo stroked on back to his seat with a look directed at me that said this is exactly the kind of treatment a foreigner could expect. But he was wrong because when my name was called followed by B+, not only did I get a few decent cat-calls from the guys, but Mrs. Clarke gave me a chocolate like everyone else. That's right, I was just like everyone else–until Mrs. Clarke opened her mouth, "It looks as though a foreigner has a better grasp of the language than some of you."

On my way back to my seat, Alfredo whistled the Star Spangled Banner, the jealous prick! The school bell rang, class was over, and Mounce, who noticed my bummed-out reaction to Mrs. Clarke's comment, slapped me on the back to try to make me feel better. "C'mon, brown-nose, if you wanna see the toughest band in the school!"

Georgie and Joanne led the pack to the gym for the monthly Friday afternoon dance. "Who gets the first dance?" Joanne asked.

"You do," Georgie answered.

"Who gets the last dance?" she asked.

"You do," he answered again. Then he reached between her legs and added, "Who gets everything in between?"

"You do," she answered, smiling.

"Fuckin' lovebirds," Mounce chuckled. "Not me, man, I like to play the field. So what was with you and Alfredo at lunch?"

"Nothing. He just wanted to know if it was really true about Eskimo women." Either Mounce accepted my explanation or he had more important things to deal with, namely being how to go from being on the outs with Georgie to being back in.

"So Georgie," he shouted, "same scam at the door?"

Georgie looked right past Mounce as if he wasn't there, and then he asked me the question I'd been anticipating all day– but at the worst possible moment: "So Steve, how'd it look this morning?"

I wanted to shout, "Just like you said, man! The look on the homeowner's face when he was trying to peel the toilet paper off his property was worth every ounce of sweat that poured off my freakin' forehead last night!" But I couldn't take the look on Mounce's face when he realized that not only had he just been snubbed by Georgie in front of everyone, but that there had been a midnight run last night that he hadn't been invited to. Now I could imagine the look on my face when Mrs. Clarke called me a foreigner in class because Mounce was wearing the same look of shame. To prevent him from feeling any worse I offered Georgie a low key "bitchin'."

If that wasn't enough humiliation to suck on, Mounce was suddenly yanked by the back of his belt. He turned around in a fit, shouting, "Hey, asshole!" . . . only to find he was face to face with Mr. Cole.

"I beg your pardon, young man, and what does that say?" The V.P. pointed to a white peroxide mark on Mounce's back pocket that read "69." "Go home and change into a clean pair of pants," he demanded. "And if I ever see that again on anything you own, you're suspended."

"But Mr. Cole, the dance . . . can't I go home after?" he pleaded.

Surprisingly, Joanne piped up: "Mr. Cole, defacing school property is definitely wrong, but shouldn't a person be able to write whatever he wants on his own personal belongings?"

"Yeah, maybe we should have a school vote, like in government," added Eddie.

A couple of the kids snickered until Mr. Cole shut them down with one of his patented scowls. "This is not your school, young man, you only attend it. When you grow up and pay taxes, then you'll earn a say in how things are run." Then he turned back to Mounce, glowering. "Why are you still here?" . . . which sent Mounce off in a huff.

Feeling sorry for Mounce, I ran to catch up to him. "The best part o' Cole dripped down his old lady's leg," Mounce said with venom. Then after a minute he asked, "Why's Georgie so pissed at me?"

It wasn't that Mounce didn't know why, it was just that he wanted confirmation; he'd been such a good friend that I couldn't lie to him.

"He thinks you didn't come into the bathroom, I mean the head, the other day . . . because you were scared. I told him it didn't happen that way." Of course, it didn't matter what I said to Mounce, being called a chicken was probably the worst thing a guy could be accused of. I searched for a way to make him feel better and what generally made Mounce feel better was whenever he explained things to me, "So tell me why was Cole pissed at you? What's '69'?"

"Six minutes, nine months, butt-head. Don't you know anything? Come on, I ain't missing this!" Mounce tore back around the corridor towards the dance with me following as usual.

To get into the dance, you had to buy a ticket from the honor students who sat at a table collecting money by the gym door. Mounce and I stood peering behind an adjacent wall to make sure Cole wasn't anywhere in sight and to watch Eddie, Georgie, Joanne, and the others who had worked their way close to the front of the line. Mounce told me we'd make our move on his signal–whatever that meant.

"Watch this," he said. As Eddie approached the table to buy his ticket from one of the Honor Nerds, Georgie and the others began to jostle him from behind.

"Hey, stop pushing back there," Eddie squawked. But the jostling continued until the crowd behind Eddie gave one giant shove and pushed him past the table and into the gym. When two of the nerds went after him to get his money, it didn't take much for Georgie and the others to surge past the remaining nerd without paying.

"Now!" Mounce ordered, and we sprinted across the hall to get swepted into the gym along with all the others. Man, you learn something new every day.

The dimly lit gym was filled with surfers, greasers, Mexicans, and nerds who quickly staked out their territories. Georgie, Joanne, Eddie, and friends elbowed their way through the crowd to hang out under the basketball net by the stage. As we passed the Mexicans, John Blakely, the class clown, did his version of "West Side Story," and everybody including Eddie Lopez laughed like hyenas. Everybody, that is, except the Mexicans.

It was crowded, but I was still worried about Mounce. "What if the V.P. catches you?" He gave me one of those looks that said he could care less. "So how come your dances are in the afternoon? Back home, ours were always at night."

Mounce made his way to the basketball net, trying to get close enough to feel part of the crowd, but far enough away that he didn't draw attention from Georgie. "Our dances were at night, too, until this girl, Mary Ellen Middleton, got raped." He said like it was no big thing. Rape was a word I heard at school every day, mostly as a joke, but it was different when you put somebody's name to it.

"Raped by who?" I asked.

"That rape artist right over there—Alfredo," answered John.

Georgie, who heard everything, turned on Mounce. "I thought Cole sent you home."

"I ain't scared of him or nobody," replied Mounce in his toughest voice.

Joanne nodded in the direction of the gym door, where Mr. Cole had just appeared. "Here's your chance to prove it," she giggled.

Georgie and the surfers joked about turning Mounce in until the lights went down and live music began to blare from the stage. The crowd hooted and hollered as the curtain opened to the sounds of The Skaggs, a five-piece instrumental band playing "Pipeline" by The Ventures.

The sight of these musicians playing in front of the whole auditorium with every eye on them was magical to me. I studied each detail, from their identical white pants and surf shirts with the broad red stripe across the chest, to their identical Fender guitars and amplifiers . . . the way each of them stood in that cool, almost bored way as if on one hand they didn't give a shit, but on the other, there was nowhere else in the universe they would rather be at that moment than here. And I felt it too, so strong that when I looked at the far end of the stage, I could see myself playing right alongside them.

"Gonna be us one day, man!" shouted Mounce, elbowing me in the ribs. I turned to give him one back and then I saw something that caught my eye, something even more incredible than the band—a girl with long red hair, staring right back at me. That's when I got the feeling that the combination of music and girls might be the most potent mixture in the world. I was hypnotized, mesmerized, stupified until something else happened to completely wipe out that awesome vision; it was the sight of Mr. Cole grabbing Mounce by the collar and dragging him out of the gym.

"Loser," Georgie chuckled.

This is how Mounce said it goes: you walk into Cole's office and he shuts the door. There is no discussion, no excuse you can make, nothing you can say to change what's going to happen next. The only words spoken are by the V.P. when he tells you to take everything out of your pockets, bend over and grab your ankles. You can't see him, but you know what he's doing, he's going to the closet to get out the weapon. You get a sense of its heft when he knocks the heavy wooden paddle against the door frame as he brings it out. That's when you see it (in your mind): big and deadly. And all the while you're bent over waiting . . . and still nothing happens. It's a trick Cole has perfected over the years. As your anticipation mounts he studies you, waiting for that precise moment when you relax your butt cheeks, and then Bam! Bam! Bam! — three whacks guaranteed to light up your ass like a Roman candle. When it's over, he tells you to stand up and put your things back in your pockets. He doesn't say a word after that and neither do you because if you did, the quiver in your voice would betray the fact that he'd gotten to you. So you straighten up and pray the tears stay way back in your head until you've left his office and gotten far enough away from anyone who might see you cry.

# CHAPTER 18

## THE PRESENT

On the way home from court, I caught the full fury of my wife's anger and frustration. She needed to vent, and who could blame her? When she finished, I said only that I did what I had to do to stop Todd and his friends from bullying Daniel. I was sorry about the consequences, but it would have been worse if I didn't do something.

"You don't know that for sure," she argued. "You're only basing that on what you went through as a teenager. These are not the same kids or the same circumstances, Steven; you . . ."

"Bullies are the same no matter when or where you

find them," I countered.

". . . cannot win a battle that happened over thirty years ago," she continued.

"You have no idea what went on back then."

"How could I?" she exclaimed. "You never talk about it. My God, I feel like I'm living with some sort of war veteran with flashbacks. Do you need professional help or something?"

"Do you even care, or should I just take some drugs and hope it all goes away?" I shot back.

From this point it could have gone either way —bloodshed or peace. We both took a breath and waited for the other to speak.

"Alright," she said, her anger depleted. "Let's have it. Let's have it all."

# CHAPTER 19

1963

"... baruch utah adonai elohenu melech ha-olim." Another night at the kitchen table going over my Bar Mitzvah prayers in front of my parents. Ever since the day I was born, I had been told we Jews were the "chosen people," but I was just now beginning to learn what that meant.

For me and Jewish kids like me all over the world, it meant the torture of having to learn our Bar Mitzvah portions in Hebrew (a foreign language for most of us) and recite them in a synagogue in front of the whole congregation on a chosen Saturday morning. You'd think that would be enough, but for me, this was a special kind of hell because no matter how I recited my prayers, it was either wrong or not good enough for my father.

"If you think I'm saying them wrong then tell me how to say them right," I barked.

"I'm not going to tell you. It's your job to know," he shot back.

"Okay, then I guess I'll have to wait 'til the Rabbi corrects me next time,"

"No you won't," he argued. "That's a lazy man's excuse. You'll do it now."

"How? Please explain to me how I should do it now? You won't tell me the right pronunciation, the Rabbi's not here to help me; maybe God will drop by and give me a lesson himself." I knew I was very close to getting a back-hand from my dad, but I didn't care because something was not making sense to me and I was frustrated. "Maybe if you told me what the words mean . . ."

"That's not the point," Dad said. "The point is to get it right."

"How do you even know it's not right?"

"Because I say so!" he shouted.

And that's when I got this image of logic flying out the window like a bat fleeing a broom-wielding crone in a hair net. There was more arguing but we were both tired and angry, and way past getting anything right. Now it was just about who was going to win. Mom tried to cool us down but it was no use; in the end, I stormed out of the kitchen and went to my room. The last thing I heard my mother say to my father was, "Why don't you try telling him *why* you can't help him, *why* it has to be perfect?" I listened, but didn't hear him give her any answer.

The only place I felt good those days was in Mounce's garage. It was a crowded, stuffy place with a work bench, a bunch of worn-out tires piled in the back, and bags filled with garbage. But with the door closed and a single light hanging over our heads, it was magic, because this was where our band practiced. And we're good, too, just as good as The Skaggs, except without the equipment, the band outfits, and the audience. There was me on acoustic guitar, Mounce, who kind of half-sat on a chair in front of his cymbal and snare (after getting his ass reamed), and our bass player, Ronnie, who never said much of anything–most bass players don't. I decided to take Vicki's advice to be unique, so we only copied the Beatles. And we would have been just as good as them, too, if we only stopped arguing and got down to practicing.

"Play slower, you're rushing," I complained to Mounce.

"Don't tell me to play slower. I'm the drummer, sing faster." And on it went, until Mounce finally threw open the garage door and stomped out into the blinding sun. The only thing I could do was to run after him and try to bring him back, while Ronnie kept playing.

"What the hell, Mounce? You don't walk out of a practice. That's not professional."

Do you notice how sometimes when you never get an answer to your question, it's not because there is no answer, it's because you're asking the wrong question? After a little prodding, I found out that Mounce was not angry so much about the music or even me trying to boss him around.

"You think you're better 'n me, doncha?" he yelled.

"No, it's just that I listen to the music and that's how the tempo feels, but if you really wanna try it your way . . ."

"You think you're in with Georgie 'cause he took you on one of his midnight runs? You don't know who you're dealin' with, man. You don't know nothin' about nothin'."

He was wrong, of course. I did know. I knew exactly what it was like to feel rejected, to feel like an outcast, and I knew that was how he felt at that moment. What I didn't know was that Mounce was also trying to tell me something that I didn't get. It was like he was giving me an answer to a question I hadn't asked, and I hadn't asked the question because I wasn't ready to hear the answer–if that makes any sense. The truth was that he was right; I was way too caught up in the feeling of being in with the in-crowd.

In the meantime, three girls had stopped to watch Ronnie. I elbowed Mounce and we all got back to playing the song, slower this time. Maybe I'd think about what he said later. But right now, I was getting that intoxicating feeling of girls mixed with music again.

There was so much to learn at Christopher Columbus Junior High School that sometimes I had to learn things twice. I'm not talking about subjects like English, math, and history, but the things you'd learn outside of class, such as bathroom or head etiquette, and not just knowing what to do when you're in there, but more importantly when to go–and by that I mean knowing who is in the head ahead of you and who is coming in after you. This was something I should've learned the time I saw Georgie get jumped.

When I stopped to take a wizz between classes, Manuello and Lupe followed me in. I didn't even notice them until I'd finished, but by then it was too late. When I went to wash my hands Manuello pulled my shirttails out of my pants so I laughed nervously, hoping they were just playing. I stuffed my shirt back in my pants and took out my comb to fix my hair.

"Not like that, man, like this," advised Manuello as he wet his own comb under the tap and brushed it through my hair – grease style.

"That's not how I do it," I replied.

"Is now," he said. Then Lupe grabbed me from behind and Manuello pushed my head under the tap.

"Cut it out!" I sputtered.

"Or what?" Manuello gestured for Lupe to let me up, then he slurped a mouth full of water out of the tap, and spit it in my face. "I choose you off, punk!" Lupe shoved me against the mirror, waiting for me to retaliate. If I had shoved him back, it would have been two against one and I would have been a dead man. If I didn't . . .

"Hey, Canada, you're gonna make these guys late for class." A toilet flushed and Alfredo emerged from of one of the stalls.

"The punk chose off Manuello, man," said Lupe. Nobody in this room believed that. Nobody in the whole wide world would have believed that. What they were really doing was asking Alfredo for his permission to take me apart, and all I knew was that whatever Alfredo wanted to happen next, would.

"Maybe if you apologized for picking on Manuello," Alfredo suggested to me, "he might let it slide."

Manuello laughed long and hard at that one. "Yeah, promise not to pick on me no more," he cracked.

If this was Alfredo's way of giving me a way out, I was happy to take it. "Sorry for picking on you, Manuello." He and Lupe laughed like jackals as they strutted out of the head, and I started to breathe again.

I don't know why Alfredo spared me the beating that

day, but I was thankful and I told him so. He responded coldly, "Don't thank me. And don't be a pussy, be a man."

TODAY I AM A MAN

# CHAPTER 20

*Be a man.* That was the phrase I heard a lot these days from my friends, from my parents, and I was sure it was the same for every kid my age from Africa to Australia–*be a man.* The question we kids were all asking was, how? You'd think the Rabbi teaching me my *haftorah* would have known, but it wasn't something you could come right out and ask. Maybe the answer was hidden somewhere in my *parsha* (the portion of my prayers), but I was having trouble enough trying to memorize it, let alone worry about what it all meant. And then one day, a miracle happened, and the Rabbi just came out with it.

"Do you know what it means, Steven, to be a Bar Mitzvah, to be a man?"

No, Rabbi, I thought to myself. And I think I speak for

every thirteen year-old boy when I say I have not the first clue who I am, what I'm doing here, or what comes next. All I know is that I can't wait to grow up, stop making the same stupid mistakes over and over again, and getting shit for it. What I do want to know is how to get my father off my back. I also want to know about girls – or at least how to get them. I want respect, I want the power and the glory, and I want the keys to the fucking kingdom! So tell me, oh bearded one, what is the big fat fucking secret?

"Steven, it's not the words that are important as much as the spirit of those words," he began. "Becoming Bar Mitzvah means your parents are no longer responsible for your actions. You alone are accountable to your community, your faith, and yourself. That's where you have to strive for perfection. Everything else is just window dressing."

That sounded good to me, and in fact when I got back in the car on our drive home I laid this wisdom on my father.

"I don't care what the Rabbi says, it *is* the words. The Rabbi is not your father. I am and your father wants it perfect."

"But why? Why's it gotta be so perfect?" I argued, "Because you were perfect when you were a kid? So now I have to be? What, did you get a gold medal or something for being The Best Little Mister Bar Mitzvah Boy? Well I'm not you, so stop expecting me to be."

I knew I was asking for it, but I didn't care anymore, I

didn't ask to be born Jewish; I didn't ask to be born at all! I didn't believe in this stupid ritual, I didn't even know if I believed in God! I was just frustrated as hell and didn't care if I got walloped for it. But just when I thought I was going to see stars from my father, my mother interrupted in a strangely quiet voice.

"You should be thankful for getting the opportunity. Some boys never get a Bar Mitzvah."

"Yeah? Name one,"

I had them now. Every kid got bar mitzvah'd whether he liked it or not. At least I thought I had them until my mother continued, "Dad's father died before he was thirteen. His family didn't have much money and lessons were expensive."

So that's why he couldn't pronounce the Hebrew words. He never had a Bar Mitzvah! He'd only heard the prayers when his friends had theirs, he never got to say them himself.

"When you become Bar Mitzvah, Steven," she continued, "it'll be for the both of you, understand?"

I caught my father looking back at me in the car mirror and I thought maybe now I did understand. I was also learning that the road to becoming a man was easier to walk once you . . . what was that phrase, "you don't know where you're going until you know where you've been"? Knowing now what I had just learned about my father, I didn't mind working a little harder; I even wanted to. And I told myself that even if it wasn't perfect, it would be alright.

As if confirming my feelings, Dad came into my room that night and handed me a box. In it was my own *tallis* (prayer shawl) because, he said, every man should have his own. Then he dropped another surprise on me, winked, and left. It was a manual of some kind. What now? Was he expecting me to become the Rabbi he never was? I picked up the book and read the title: *What Every Teenager Should Know About Sex*. The road to becoming a man was one twisted journey.

# CHAPTER 21

Georgie, and Eddie and I were at the corner store and I was trying to explain the whole Bar Mitzvah thing to them, but they were not getting it.

"So you wear this little beanie and shawl and you sing a few prayers and that's it? You're officially a man?" asked Eddie.

"What it really means is that I'm responsible for my own actions."

"Like graduatin' from Juvee Hall to adult court, huh?" cracked Georgie. Then it suddenly hit him, "Jeez, I thought we only had to worry about the Mexicans. Now we got a Jew in school."

Faint warning bells began to ring in my head, as Eddie added, "Better that than the niggers downtown." Back home there weren't any Negroes in our school, but still, we never used that word. It was like calling a Jew a kike, and you'd never hear that in my neighborhood. What I didn't understand was why a Mexican who hated being called a beaner would call black people niggers. Anyway, even if they called me a Jew, it's not like they called me a *dirty* Jew.

Apart from that, the guys were all for helping me become a man, or at least their version of a man. Eddie looked around and stuffed a fistful of candy bars in his shirt while Georgie shoved a pack of cigarettes and a Playboy magazine down the back of his pants. Then as they headed out the door they give me the look that told me it was my turn. I'd never stolen anything in my life before but I had a feeling that if I didnt, it wouldn't be long before I'd be hearing, "dirty Jew coward." As I reached for a candy bar, the store manager walked up to me. He was a big man, over 200 pounds. His name tag read "Norm," and the way he asked if he could help me sounded like code for, "Don't even think about stealing that candy bar, kid."

The boys waited in the shadows by the edge of the parking lot until I came out and joined them empty-handed. Georgie pulled out his stolen pack of cigarettes and Eddie grabbed for one, but Georgie slapped his hand.

"Ask nice," Georgie demanded.
"Fuck you," Eddie replied.

"That's better." And Georgie offered him a cigarette.

"Fuck you, too," I repeated just like Eddie, but no cigarette was offered. I knew they were thinking that I was a chickenshit because I didn't get away with anything, so I explained that the manager was wise to us all and, in fact, I distracted him so both Georgie and Eddie could get away. It seemed to work and I got my smoke and everything was cool until Georgie started flipping through the Playboy and I met my next challenge to manhood.

"Jeez, I'd like to 69 her," Georgie snickered. I nodded my agreement which was when the trouble started.

"You don't even know what it means," Eddie smirked.

"Sure he does," Georgie said, defending me. "Steve's gonna be a man soon. Hey, you're in tight with Vicki Bowden, aren't you?"

I bragged that not only am I in tight with her but she was coming over tonight to baby-sit my little brother and sister. But as soon as I'd said it, I knew I'd said too much, so I quickly added that my folks wouldn't let me have friends over if they weren't home–just so they knew they couldn't drop over. Eddie told me I was full of shit about being tight with Vicki and dared me to prove it by asking her to come out for a walk. Jesus, I should've just stolen the goddamn candy bar and kept my big mouth shut.

Twenty minutes later, Vicki, Georgie, Eddie, and I

were strolling down the block together, watching the hazy sun set over the San Fernando hills. Georgie offered Vicki a cancer stick and to my surprise she accepted it. As Georgie went on about all the friends they had in common from school, I could see why girls and guys liked him–he had the gift. Even the cigarette in his mouth seemed to enjoy hanging out with him, and for the moment so did I. But the moment passed.

"So, my friend Steven is gonna be a man in a couple o' weeks and he wants to know what 69 means."

"I know! I know what it is!" Did I come off too confident or too desperate? Jesus, why did he even have to say anything?

"Oh yeah? What is it then?" Eddie piped up.

Now it wasn't that I didn't know, because Mounce already told me, but it was a topic you didn't discuss in front of a young lady. Not that anything I said or did at this point was going to help avoid the disaster to which we were clearly headed.

"Don't worry about Vicki," Georgie purred. "She knows all about it, doncha, Vicki?" If she did, she was not saying. Or maybe silence was her way of telling Georgie that she was no pushover. If that was the way she wanted to play it, that was fine with me because I was no pushover either. I'd show them all this time because this time I had the answer.

"Six minutes, nine months!" I declared, as if I'd read it

right out of the American Constitution. I'm not sure why, but Georgie and Eddie nearly fell down laughing. Even Vicki tried to hide a giggle . . . and then I got it–Mounce was wrong! I wanted to dig myself a hole all the way to China and dive into it. When Georgie finally pulled himself together he took a stick and sketched the number in the dirt.

"That's her head and your thing, right? And that's your head and her thing, right?" I nodded, yes, as I mentally fast-forwarded through every page of that stupid manual my father gave me, but I could not remember a single sketch or reference to this infamous number. By now it was so painfully obvious to everyone that I was a sexual retard that in the spirit of making me a man (or a laughing stock), Georgie turned to Vicki and said, "What he really needs is a demonstration." Just then Vicki remembered that she had a test to study for and left to go home. "It'll only take a minute!" he called out.

"Or six!" shouted Eddie, and they both laughed until they just about choked.

"What did you have to do that for?" I raged after Vicki was gone.

"We didn't do anything, man. You just got some bad information and we were trying to help you out is all," pleaded Georgie.

"Who told you that shit anyway, Mounce?" asked Eddie, rubbing it in.

Now it was my turn to tell them that I had to go home to study, which is exactly what I did–buried my nose in that stupid sex manual and looked for the vital information, but it wasn't there–thanks for nothing, Dad!

It's funny how when you're far from home, the little things you either never took notice of or hated to do before, suddenly become so important, like sitting down for dinner and talking about your day. As kids, we never gave it a second thought. Meals just used to interrupt our play time. But with all the moving and adjusting, I could see how those silly family traditions helped keep a sense of who we were. My mother was not good with change, so she did everything she could to keep things normal, like using the same dishes she used back home and making the same food for our meals. She would holler at us every night to come to dinner and we'd all sit down and eat while she managed to serve the whole family including my baby sister.

But things change no matter how hard you try to keep them the same. For example, my sister was more interested now in throwing food than eating it. My previously shy four-year-old brother Dustin wouldn't shut up–as if being part of a family gave him the right to voice his opinion on everything whether it had to do with him or not. Still he was not as big a pain in the ass as my other brother, Paul, (the devil child) whose dedication to tormenting me had just about become a religious calling. It got so bad that Mom had him meet with a special doctor. When they got home, I overheard her telling Dad that the doctor said that Paul acts out so much because it was the only way he could get attention. So his advice was to praise Paul for anything positive we could find.

"Thanks, Paul, for putting your plate in the sink." "Paul, that was nice of you to give your sister a turn to watch her T.V. program." "Paul, when you're finished sticking that knife into your brother's stomach, please put it back in the drawer where you found it, there's a good boy."

When Paul made it onto the school football team, my folks treated him like he'd been drafted to the majors . . . and guess what? Slowly, it began to work. He became nicer and a lot easier to get along with. I guess there was a lesson here for me, too. I mean, life was going to happen and I'd have to face whatever challenges came my way, whether I was in Toronto or Los Angeles. So maybe if I approached my problems in a more mature way, I'd get the answers I needed, and what better time to ask them than at the dinner table, when everybody was together?

"So Mom, Dad, the guys and I were having a little discussion today about this sex act they call 69? I mean, I know it's about sex but exactly what kind of sex is it? Is it the kind you make babies from, or is it the dirty kind? Or is all sex dirty? I'm just asking because when the subject came up I was a little embarrassed about not having the correct answer and I know Dad likes me to be perfect at everything. I even looked it up in the manual he gave me, but honestly, I couldn't find a thing on the fucking subject, so I thought if you could explain it to me here at the dinner table I wouldn't have to embarrass myself in front of my friends anymore. And, in fact, maybe if we got it all out in the open now, my brothers and sister wouldn't have to go through the same embarrassment when their turn came. So why don't we jump into it all, starting with this 69 thing and the first question I have is what happened to everything from 1 on up to that magic number, because I read the manual from front to back and never once did I see the '69 steps of love.' And after you've answered that one, maybe you can clear something else up for me: like when you're with a girl, are you actually supposed to start at 1 and work your way up to 69 (which to me sounds like a lot of work)? And if so, how is a guy supposed to remember every damn step? It sounds harder than trying to memorize the times tables. I mean before you begin, do you write it all on your arm or bring a cheat sheet to bed with you?

    Oh, and then what happens *after* 69? What if my girlfriend gets tired of everything and she wants to go to 70? Is there a different set of instructions for that, and if there is, then how high up does this bloody thing go, and how you do you know you're finished, Mom and Dad, because to tell you the truth, sex is starting to sound like a lot more work than it's worth!"

I was sure I'd get my answers if I only had the guts to ask the question out loud, but instead I just sat sullenly through dinner and went back to my room to study.

A short time later I heard my parents giving last minute instructions to Vicki before they went out for the evening. "We're going out to a movie, Vicki, be back by twelve."

Jeez, how could I face her now after making such a fool of myself earlier? Better to hide out in my room and study my haftorah for the rest of the night. Later, I heard Vicki put Honey into her crib and tuck Dustin into bed. I switched from studying to playing guitar, which helped me ignore the fact that she was just a few feet away. Bad move, 'cause a minute later there was a knock at my door. I played louder to drown her out but the door opened anyway and there she was. All I could do was keep on playing and try to ignore the burning pain in the tips of my fingers that pressed so hard against the frets, a pain that could not compare to that of facing Vicki who must have thought by now that I was some kind of sexual moron . . . oh God, please don't let her see the sex manual on my dresser . . . fingers cramping up, so raw that they're gonna bleed . . . God give me strength to keep playing until she walks out . . . whatever you do, don't let her see the manual . . .

"It's not in there, you know." she said, nodding at the book. "But if you want, I'll tell you."

Now the last thing any guy wanted was a girl lecturing him about sex. If anything, it should be the guy making the girl do things she doesn't want to do, am I right? Not only that, but just the sheer embarrassment of *talking* about it . . . I mean you should be *doing* it with a girl, not talking about it. And with the lights off! The way I heard it, the less communication, the better. Anyway, Vicki took a seat next to me on the bed and lowered her voice to a whisper, I guess so the kids down the hall wouldn't hear.

"It all starts when a guy and a girl are kissing and fooling around and he gets a stiffy."

Oh God! Then as she described all the twisting and turning of the bodies and the mechanics of what 69 really was, which not only flipped my world upside down, but made me wonder whether she was putting me on or what. I mean, these were the same organs you go to the bathroom with, so who in their right mind would put them in their mouths? Not my parents, that's for sure! I couldn't even take a bite out of an apple without my mother shouting, "Did you wash that?" If what Vicki told me was really true, then between beer, cigarettes, and all the weird sex, adulthood sounded like one big disgusting experience after another. And yet for some strange reason, the very things that sounded so gross, were getting me horny. Maybe it was the combination of her voice and the closeness of her body, the smell of her perfume, and all the talk (man, she had to know I was picturing *me* on top of *her* at that moment) . . . oh God, did her hand just touch mine? Was she going to take it and put it on her? Was she telling me all this because she really wanted me to 69 her now, right here in my bedroom?

That's when I heard the scream–not from her or from me, but from down the hall. Vicki and I both jumped up and raced into the den where Paul stared bug-eyed out the glass patio window doors where someone who was dressed in bloody bandages was trying to get in! Vicki rushed to the door to make sure it was locked. Then, just like in a horror movie, there was another banging noise coming from the kitchen. We were under attack! Was the kitchen door locked?

"Don't leave me!" cried Paul.

My brother grabbed me by my shirt and all three of us ran into the kitchen where a second bloody figure banged away at the door — only this door was unlocked. Then, as if reading my mind, the intruder turned the knob and entered.

"Get out of here! I'm calling the Cops!" Vicki screamed.

"Get out of here! I'm calling the Cops!" the intruder screamed back. Then he broke into a nasty laugh and unwrapped the bandages from his face. It was Georgie. A second later, Eddie came running up behind him, unraveling his bandages too.

"Relax, sweet tits, we just dropped by for a little fun," he cackled.

Vicki picked up the phone and threatened to make a call. "Not as long as I'm here!"

"You're not really going to call the cops," said Georgie.

"Nope, I'm calling my Dad. He's right next door. You saw him last week, didn't you? Big guy."

"Okay, okay. How about a glass of water then?" sighed Georgie. "It's hot in these bandages," Vicki shook her head, no, and when the boys didn't leave, she started dialing.

"Cool it, we were only razzing our buddy. See you at school, Steve," said Georgie.

"Sleep tight. Don't let the boogeyman bite," added Eddie as the two left.

Vicki locked the kitchen door after them while I tried to calm my brother down. "It was only a joke, okay? You gotta promise us, Paul, not to tell Mom and Dad."

"They coulda hurt us, or killed us," he whimpered.

I remembered what my mother said about giving Paul all the positive reassurance he needed. "Number one, you were very brave, though they wouldn't have hurt us because they're friends of mine from school. Second, it's Dad's dream to come here to Los Angeles and if we mess it up for him it'll be our fault, understand? And you were very brave." It looked like I might be getting through to him, but he wasn't stupid, and I wondered if my little brother had already figured out that because they were *my* friends, that whatever punishment came of this would fall on my head.

Vicki took a different approach at getting my brother on-side. "Hey Paul, how about a big bowl of ice cream?"

After the ice cream we all walked down the hall together to make sure the two younger ones were still asleep and then we put Paul to bed. Vicki and I glanced at the spot where we almost 'did it' and smiled, friends again. Maybe more.

Today I am a Man

# CHAPTER 22

  One of the most popular hang-outs at school was the sand pit where the guys would show off their skills on the monkey bars. The first thing everyone learned was the kip-up, which got you onto the bars and into position for everything else. You started by grabbing hold of the bars above you and swinging your legs back and forth until you got enough momentum to whip them out in front of you. Then you used the downward thrust to propel your body up so that your hips ended up level with the bar. From there, you could go into hip circles, layouts, fly-aways and full circles. Georgie was the king of the bars. At fourteen, he already had the lean muscular build of an athlete. Others may have been better at muscle-ups but no one could touch Georgie when he glided from a swing to kip-up to layout in one smooth motion.

"It was just a hazing," he shouted from on top of the bar. "It's like an initiation all our friends get, right, John?" John nodded along with some of the others who had already heard about last night.

Georgie continued, "In fact, if we didn't like you, we wouldn't have bothered doing it at all. It took a lot of work putting that shit together, ya know. Besides, nobody got hurt, right?" I nodded my agreement. Besides, if I didn't shrug it off, I wouldn't be hanging out here much longer.

To show that we were still friends, Georgie dismounted and gestured for me to grab the bars. "Put your hands here and then swing," he instructed. Then he pushed me until I built momentum and then John got on the other side of me to assist. "Now whip your legs down and pull your body up at the same time."

When I'd swung my legs out far enough they grabbed me by the hips and pulled them into the bar. I extended my arms, and there I was on top of the world.

"There ya go!" shouted Georgie like a proud papa.

"When we pulled that on Mounce a few months ago, he nearly shit his pants," said Eddie.

Mounce, who was sitting at the edge of the pit, gave me a look that reminded me of his warning a few days ago: "You don't know who you're dealin' with, man. You don't know nothin' about nothin'."

Joanne and a few of the girls came wandering over. They were generally not very far from sight anyway (always on the lookout for other girls cutting in on their territory), but this time the talk sounded important, as if they were on a mission. In fact they were. Tracy's folks were going out of town this weekend and the girls were trying to talk her into hosting a party. If they succeeded, they'd score big with the guys, which was the reason they were talking it up at the pit. Suddenly my hazing had become old business.

"If I do, it's not going to be an open party, okay?" said Tracy. "I don't want any greasers showing up and starting trouble. Georgie, think you can you get The Skaggs to play?" I learned that every social thing here had to go through Georgie. He decided if there would be a party or not, what kind of entertainment there would be, and who would be invited. Georgie didn't say no to asking The Skaggs, so it looked like the party was on. With a nod of Georgie's head, everyone started in with who was on the invitation list, and who would bring what.

When the inevitable subject of liquor came up, Mounce, who had been quiet until now, piped in. "I can steal some from my old man's liquor cabinet, easy."

"Chicken-shits ain't invited," Eddie shot back. The crowd went silent. This was a definite slap-down, a challenge that had to be met.

"You think I'm a chicken-shit, Eddie? yelled Mounce. "I choose you off, man!" Mounce knew he was way out of his league and so did everyone else, but everyone hadn't seen a good fight since Georgie took on Alfredo.

Joanne whispered something to Georgie, who turned to Mounce. "Sit down, Mounce," he ordered. By saying this, Georgie had just done two things; he'd told Eddie to back off, and he has given Mounce an excuse to stomp off in a righteous fit, acting pissed for not getting a chance to defend his honor. And thanks to Joanne, Mounce was saved from getting his ass kicked. I would have figured Eddie to be pissed off about it, but he just smiled at the whole business. Eddie was a queer one, one of those guys who loved to stir things up just to watch the shit fly. You could be his best friend one second and his enemy the next. There never seemed to be a rhyme or reason except that the guy loved trouble. The only person who had the power to bring this mongrel to heel was Georgie. I guess you had to respect Georgie for at least that.

When the school bell rang and we headed to class, I caught up to Tracy to ask her if Mounce could come to her party, reminding her that he did offer to bring the drinks. After she hmm'd and haw'd a bit, she said that as long as it was okay with Georgie, it was cool with her–big surprise. Great, off I went to shop class.

One thing schools were really big on here were the shop classes; not that they didn't have them back home, but those were mainly for the kids who had pretty well decided not to go to university. The main reason we didn't have them in Canada, I think, is because our teachers were worried that some goof would hurl a spitball at some other goof and cause him to lose a finger. But in L.A., either they weren't worried about losing digits or they weren't worried about losing goofs because there were all kinds of e-limb-inator shops around–car shop, metal shop, plastics shop. My favorite was print shop because we got to work on our own personal projects and mine was printing band cards. This was also where I'd find Georgie.

When I got to class, I put on my apron, went to my cubby, and got the bracket that held the metal type in place for my business card. I looked around for Georgie, who was a few presses down, working on his project. You'd think you'd find him in car shop or something but he was actually the best artist in the class, always drawing pictures of people, cars, and surfers. His current project was designing a flyer with a cartoon of himself with a caption that read, "Wanted Dead Or Alive"–what a sense of humor. While Georgie was starting to ink up the press I figured this was the best time to approach him. I ambled on down to check out his work.

"Nice work, Georgie. You ever take art classes, 'cause you're really talented?" He shook his head, no. "So this party

Tracy is having sounds pretty cool." I got a nod and I figured I'd softened him up enough. "Georgie, I know you think Mounce was chicken for not coming to help you fight Alfredo the other day in the head, but I dunno . . . I mean, he was way behind me in the corridor, we weren't even walking together when it happened so chances are he never even saw what I saw. Plus a few minutes ago you saw how he wasn't afraid to stand up to Eddie . . ."

"Somebody chooses you off, you got no choice," proclaimed Georgie as if it was the Gospel.

It was hard to know if I was getting through, but he hadn't said no yet. "Look, I know I'm new here and I don't know that much, but when somebody stands up to somebody else *knowing* he's probably going to get his ass kicked, wouldn't that prove he's not a chicken?"

Georgie stopped inking his press and looked at me. Did I go too far, did I piss him off? A little grin broke out on his face. I guess I must have convinced him because he agreed to let Mounce come to the party–on one condition. As I returned to my press and my band cards, I wondered if I was as smart as I thought I was, or if had I stuck my hand in the proverbial press to save my project, only to lose a finger.

After school I raced over to Mounce's house to give him the good news and show him our cards, which had a picture of three Medieval knights in one corner, my phone number in the other corner, and the name of our band, The Vulcans, right across the top. I was really proud of it. But instead of complimenting me, the first thing out of Mounce's mouth was, "Why *your* number?"

"Because I'm the one who made up the cards and because I got you into Tracy's party."

As I handed him the cards I explained how I arranged everything, and even though I could see he was excited, I also sensed he had some worries. Knowing Georgie all too well, Mounce wanted to know what this little favor cost, but I told him that I just got Georgie at a good time, that's all. I don't know if he believed me or not but he thanked me anyway with a "Bitchin, man!"–then his mother shouted from the other room, warning him not to use that language in the house and that dinner was ready. Having done my good deed for the day, I trotted home to my dinner. Now all I had to do was to find a way to keep my end of my bargain with Georgie.

TODAY I AM A MAN

# CHAPTER 23

*"Bond's hand was on her left breast. Its peak was hard with passion. Her stomach pressed against his. Why not? Why not? Don't be a fool! This is a crazy time for it. You're both in deadly danger. You must stay cold as ice to have any chance of getting out of this mess."*

Vicki and I were sitting cross-legged in the bamboo thicket out in my backyard reading a passage from *Doctor No*. It was dark outside so I brought a flashlight whose beam occasionally drifted from the page to Vicki's chest–by accident. Either she didn't notice or she didn't care, but in any case, I had to keep a clear head because, like Bond, I was on a mission, a mission to uphold my part of the bargain with Georgie–to get Vicki to come to Tracy's party.

Why Vicki was sitting here in the first place was a mystery to me. Most girls didn't hang out with younger guys; they'd rather be with the older ones, that much even I knew. Maybe she liked younger guys, and if she did, did she like me enough to do me this favor? But if she did me this favor would that mean I was using her? Damn Georgie for putting me in a position where I have to use one friend to help another. How do I choose which one is more important? On the one hand, Mounce had taught me more about surviving school than anyone else I'd met. On the other, Vicki was everything pure and beautiful, and might be the best thing about this whole trip to L.A. It looked like no matter what choice I made it was bound to be the wrong one. I had a feeling not even James Bond could have gotten out of this.

And if that wasn't enough to deal with, Vicki was driving me crazy as she continued to read, *"He rubbed his face against hers and then brought his mouth round to hers and gave her one long kiss."* God, why was she doing this to me? Was she trying to torture me or was I so dense that I didn't realize that what she was reciting was what she really wanted me to do, take her face in my hands and kiss her? Who was I kidding, I'd be a jerk to make a move on her and only make a bigger fool of myself. Better to stick to the plan and just tell her what Georgie wanted, let her make the decision, and then it would be out of my hands. But I was in agony sitting next to her, smelling her hair and her Pepsodent-fresh breath, listening to her speak these forbidden words that passed through those pomegranate lips like exotic travelers on a journey to worlds I yearned to know, from a place I had never felt before inside me. Jesus, did that just come out of me? This must be love! I was gonna do it, I was going to put my hands on her and kiss her, and then after I'd know that I could never sacrifice her for anyone, not even my best friend, Mounce, and together, Vicki and I would travel to those places that existed only for lovers. But before I made my move the patio door opened and my mom called me. Our journey of love would have to wait. I motioned with my flashlight for Vicki to stay where she was until I found out what my mother wanted. When I emerged from my bamboo hideout, I found I was facing not only my mother, but my father, and my rat fink brother, Paul.

"We want to talk to you about your friends who came over the other night, mister."

*I must stay cold as ice to have any chance of getting out of this mess.*

The next day in the cafeteria line, I bitched to Mounce, who was the only one who would understand. "I nearly got grounded 'cause of that stupid prank Georgie and Eddie pulled the other night, and it wasn't even my fault. I almost couldn't go to Tracy's party."

"I told you about Georgie, man, but the other side of

the coin is that unless you knew him you wouldn't be going to the bitchin'est party of the year." He was right. Being friends with Georgie was like being friends with some kind of weird two-headed beast.

And if that wasn't enough for me to brood over, the red-haired girl I saw at the school dance was standing just ahead of me in line. Mounce followed my gaze. "That's Sherry. Wanna meet her?"

Why would I wanna meet Sherry when I'm in love with Vicki? Not that anything would ever come out of either girl knowing me. In truth I was no Georgie, so why bother taking the risk? It was better to not try, than to get shot down in front of the whole school.

"She's not so hot. Besides, Mounce, you don't just walk up and introduce someone to a girl like some dope. It's not cool."

"It ain't me who's the dope, so who cares?" Then he dragged me past a couple of nerds in line and pushed me right into Sherry. "Sorry," he apologized. "It's just my friend, Steve, here hasn't eaten in days. His folks keep him locked up in the cellar 'til it's time for school."

This was not how James Bond would have approached a woman, but I guess here at Christopher Columbus Junior High School, it worked because she giggled. "Ask her to the party," Mounce whispered.

"Are you crazy, I don't even know her."

But Mounce had a solution for everything: he grabbed a pastry and tossed it on her tray. "This is from Steve, he loves Sherry pie," and whispered to me, "At least, you do now," Then he moved off to give us some privacy. I could see by the look on her face that Mounce's crass play had closed the book on any interest she might have in me, that is, until Georgie passed by and slapped me on the back as if to say, "top of the morning, dude." Incredibly, it worked, because Sherry's eyes were actually glimmering.

"You're the new kid aren't you? From Canada?" she asked.

"Yeah," I answered with a little more confidence. "Sorry about Mounce, sometimes he just . . ." Sherry nodded and I nodded—a silent understanding between us that Mounce could be a jerk sometimes. And then I realized that this was exactly what Mounce intended all along: to act like a jerk in order to make me look good in front of her. Sometimes, he was wise way beyond his years.

"Anyways, this girl Tracy is having a party this weekend and I thought, maybe, if you weren't busy, you'd like to go?" Sherry smiled, wrote her phone number on my hand, then moved off to buy her lunch and sit with her friends. I guess I owed Mounce for that, and in a way I owed Georgie too, which I have a feeling was only going to complicate

## Today I am a Man

things later.

# CHAPTER 24

"I'm In With The In Crowd" was one of the bossest songs in those days but my parents hated it because I played it all the time on my hi-fi. Dressed in my new surf shirt with the big red stripe across the chest, white pants and socks, I tossed my hair to get that windswept look and felt ready for the bitchin'est party of the year. I thought I looked pretty good but it never hurt to get a second opinion from your mother. I wandered around the house and found her putting my baby sister to bed.

"Who is that good-looking young man?" she said brightly.

Mothers, they always know exactly what you need when you need it. Satisfied, I went looking for my Dad next, who agreed to drive Sherry and me to the party. He was the one I really wanted to get the nod from, and I found him in the den watching some program on T.V. about the Vietnam War while my brothers played with their erector sets on the floor nearby. And then it became clear to me: There were two worlds existing together in this same room, the world of children and toys, and the world of grown-ups. I stepped over my brothers to be with my Dad, easy as pie. He acknowledged me with a nod but instead of telling me how good I looked, he made some comment about the T.V. program.

"Remember the Cuban Missile Crisis, Steven," he asked, "when Khrushchev wanted to put missiles in Cuba to scare the U.S. but Kennedy circled the island with battle ships and scared the Russians off instead? Same thing here. The Communists in North Vietnam are trying to crush the democracy in South Vietnam but the U.S. is not going let that happen. Like I told you, bullies are cowards. All you have to do is stand up to them and they back down. This is some country, isn't it?"

I nodded as I watched the program with him, trying to look as concerned as he did. No, he didn't mention my clothes the way my Mom did but he did something else, he talked to me like a man, like an equal and on the night of my first date, there was nothing more I could ask for. I had stepped over my brothers and their toys, and into the world of adulthood.

It took fifteen minutes to drive over to Sherry's house, and fifteen seconds to run up to her door. She answered right way, as if she'd been waiting breathless for me all day long with her red hair done up above her little red dress, looking like a half devil, half angel. Did her parents have any idea how sexy she looked? Even my Dad looked impressed when I brought her to the car.

Ten minutes later, we pulled up to Tracy's house, one of those ranch style houses with a big round driveway and a huge front lawn. I opened the car door for Sherry but before I escorted her up the walkway Dad called me aside, out of earshot. "Now I don't have to tell you there's no smoking or drinking – and as for the girl, you treat her with respect, like a lady, you hear? Pick you up at 11:30. Have fun."

I nodded like I'd heard it a thousand times and we trooped up to Tracy's house, where we were finally on our own, literally, as we were the first ones at the party. Actually, I was glad we were here early, because it meant that I got to watch the musicians set up their equipment. Sherry sat on the couch while I peppered the band with questions. "Are all those Fender guitars? Amps, too? How much did they cost?"

It turned out that one of the guys' fathers worked for the company so figured that if I make friends with them, maybe I could get a deal when I was ready to buy my first electric guitar. I didn't know about Sherry, but I was having the time of my life and the party hadn't even started.

Tracy saw us sitting there on the couch and gave us the job of informing everyone about the house rules when they showed up. "No smoking or drinking in the house—backyard only, and if anyone gets one stain on this rug . . ."

"We can do that easy," I answered. Then she ran off to put out the potato chips and jube-jubes.

A half hour later, the place was packed, and poor Tracy was on her hands and knees picking food and cigarette butts out of the broadloom. It was a great party, that is until I spotted Georgie huddled in a corner arguing with his girlfriend, Joanne.

"Isn't that Georgie? Aren't you gonna go over and say hi?" asked Sherry.

The last thing I wanted to do was to speak to Georgie and if I was careful, I could duck him all night.

"Naw, it looks like those two are fighting, maybe later."

But I couldn't avoid Mounce, who sneaked up behind me and smacked me in the ass. "Hey you two lovebirds . . . that Ronnie, man he is such a dork. Steve, in "Satisfaction," doesn't Mick say the word 'pregnant'?"

I could hardly hear what he was saying because the music was so loud and there were so many people. If Sherry heard Mounce at all she just shrugged him off. Musician-talk wasn't for her. But one thing we all heard and saw was Georgie swearing at his girlfriend, who went running out of the house in tears.

"Those two . . ." says Mounce. ". . . they break up every week."

Tracy was almost in tears herself, watching the crowd destroy her home. She pushed her way over to Georgie and begged him to boot out the crashers, but he was only interested in another beer, that is until he spotted me and Mounce. The place was so packed that there was nowhere for me to go, and as he swaggered over to us we could see that he was not just drunk, he was plastered.

"Hey Mouncey, glad you could make it, man. And look at you two turtle doves – Sherry and Steve, made for each other." Georgie put his arm around me and whispered, "So I got your buddy in. What about your part of the bargain? Where's Vicki?"

This was the moment I was dreading but I had my excuses all prepared. "I asked her, Georgie, I swear, but she had an audition for a commercial and she told me she'd make it after, if she could."

Georgie's sloppy smile turned downright sour. "An audition on a Saturday night?"

Mounce's radar immediately picked up a danger signal and tried to shift the conversation.

"Georgie, waddya think, I've been trying to tell these dorks that Mick says 'pregnant' in "Satisfaction." Tracy, you know the song. You must have the record."

"I'm not doing anything for anybody until somebody gets these crashers out of my house!" she wailed.

Sherry excused herself to go to the bathroom and then Georgie said, "Tracy has a record player in her bedroom, trust me. Why don't you guys go check it out while I take care of everything here."

Mounce took the opportunity to whisper something to me while he dragged me down the hall. "Number one, he's drunk and when he's drunk, stay out of his way cause you never know what he'll do. Number two, what the hell did you promise him to let me come to the party?" I pretended I didn't hear him as we entered Tracy's bedroom, a world of pink shag, teddy bears, and walls filled with posters of Fabian, Troy Donahue, and Elvis Presley. But Mounce wouldn't let it go, he was like a bulldog. "What did you say you'd do? Tell me."

"Nothing. He wanted me to bring Vicki to the party and I said I'd ask her, is all."

"I told you before, you don't know who you're dealing with."

"It's not like I promised to bring her," I replied weakly. "I just said I'd try. Besides, you saw him, he's so smashed he won't even remember a thing he said tonight."

Mounce shook his head as if I was some kind of retard while he fingered Stacy's stack of 45's. He finally found the record he wanted, put it on the turntable, and laid the needle down. The famous guitar lick cranked up and Mounce raised his hand for silence until we came to the verse where he thought he heard *the notorious word*. "Hear? Hear?" he asks.

"Who can hear anything the way that guy sings?"

Mounce raised the needle and played the same section over again, but the last thing on my mind right now was The Rolling Stones. When Sherry came out of the bathroom she wouldn't know where I was, and I was responsible for her so I figured I better agree with him if I wanted to find her again.

"Okay, okay, I hear it, you're fuckin' Dick Clark. Now can we go?"

I don't know why I was so worried about Sherry, because she was sure as shit not worried about me. When I came out of Tracy's room I found her on the couch with Georgie, who was busy shoving his tongue down her throat between gulps of beer. And if that wasn't enough, Eddie Lopez was smiling at me from across the room like I was the town fool. I was so pissed that I walked right up to Eddie, ripped that grin off his face with my hands, and stomped it into the carpet with my shoe leaving another greasy stain for Tracy to wash out after her party. Then I pulled Georgie off Sherry and threw him right through the big bay window onto the front lawn. Or at least I would have, if Mounce hadn't dragged me into the kitchen and made me take a swig of beer.

"Alright, I'm gonna tell you something," he whispered, "but you gotta promise not to repeat it." I could barely concentrate, thinking of Georgie making out with my date, the girl my father told me to treat with respect. Mounce looked around to make sure no one else could hear and then he leaned in. "Remember I told you about that girl who got raped? She was walkin' home after school through the field one day, you know, where the fight was? That's where it happened. Everyone said it was a beaner, they said it was Alfredo. But I know the truth. It was Georgie."

"Bullshit, you're just saying that to make me feel better."

"No lie," he said. "I know because my dad's a lawyer and he worked on the case. It was all hushed up, like, and they used Alfredo as the 'skategoat'. Why am I telling you this? 'Cause you think you know him, but trust me, you don't."

Suddenly we heard the sound of blaring of horns outside as if God has just affirmed Mounce's story, but it wasn't God, it was Alfredo and the Mexicans. I could hear him knocking on the front door trying to get into the party, and Tracy refusing to open up. Alfredo's older brother, Ricardo, who drove him over in his car, kept pounding his horn in protest.

"Beaners! Greasers!" shouted the party-goers.

Tracy elbowed her way past a dozen kids in a panic to find four souped-up cars sitting outside her house. "Oh, my God! Oh, my God! No rumbles, no fights! Georgie?"

Georgie slid off Sherry and staggered to the window. When he saw what was waiting outside, he cracked open the window and shouted, "Sorry, man, closed party." As if the Mexicans were just going to drive away.

"Georgie, you gotta *do* something!" Tracy pleaded. "My folks are gonna kill me!" Eddie slithered over to Georgie. "You can't go out there, man, you're too loaded."

Drunk or sober, Georgie was no dummy. He took a minute to clear his head, then shouted to Alfredo. "One of ours'll take on one of yours and that'll be it, okay? That way, no cops."

The Mexicans seemed to be good with that. Georgie took another swig of beer and then slowly surveyed the room. Who was it going to be? Some of the tougher dudes like Blakely and Turner stepped up, but Georgie kept looking around until he stopped . . . at us.

Alfredo was waiting on the lawn with his legs astride and his sleeves rolled up. Tracy's door opened and Mounce walked out. He didn't have to. He was doing this for me because I was the one Georgie picked.

"This is the toughest you could find?" laughed Alfredo

along with his compadres. Georgie responded in a liquored slur. "Point is, even our smallest runt can wipe your ass."

Mounce tried to control his nerves as he called out his challenge to the toughest Mexican in the school. "C'mon, Alfredo, I . . . I choose you off!" Then Mounce raised his fists and walked down the front steps toward Alfredo with all the confidence of a condemned man.

Alfredo was more than a head taller than Mounce and twenty-five pounds heavier. No way was this a fair fight and everyone inside and out knew it, but Mounce stepped up anyway and got a lightning-quick slap in the head for his trouble. He answered with a punch at Alfredo way shy of its mark, and then the two began to circle. For whatever reason, Alfredo didn't throw any hard ones, but just continued to slap Mounce around. I don't know if that was to humiliate him or minimize his pain, but the Mexicans were laughing their heads off at this side show. And they weren't the only ones. Georgie and Eddie fell into fits of laughter every time Mounce got stung.

Eventually the show grew boring and both sides began to shout for blood. Frustrated, Manuello climbed out of the car and ran over to sock Mounce on the jaw, knocking him into the bushes. The Mexicans roared their approval. That's when Tracy picked up her phone; she knew what was going to happen next. Outside on the lawn, Manuello circled Mounce, who was on the ground kicking his legs to try to keep the Mexican at bay.

"The guy's like a fuckin' crab, man," shouted Manuello, who managed to land a few kicks to Mounce's ribs, making him wheeze. Mounce reached for his inhaler. "What's this, your secret weapon?" Manuello kicked it out of his hand and picked it up, then started pumping the gas out of the inhaler while Mounce held out his hands for it like a beggar.

As scared as I was of getting beat up, I couldn't take it anymore and shouted through the window, "Alfredo, he needs it, he could die!"

Alfredo raised his hands like it was beyond his control. But even if they thought Mounce was a punk, the surfers weren't going to let him suffer at the hands of their enemies, so they poured out of the house, the smell of blood in the air. The only one who hung back was Eddie, who never took sides.

The Mexicans piled out of their cars and charged onto the lawn, meeting the surfers for a full-fledged rumble. This was exactly what Tracy feared most. Fists and feet flew like rockets, sometimes hitting their mark, sometimes missing. I bobbed and weaved through the barrage to try to get Mounce's inhaler without getting clipped, past guys who looked like they were high on the action, like it was some kind of drug raging through their veins.

All the while I heard my mother's voice in the back of

my mind, warning me, "Get out of there! This is no place for a nice Jewish boy!" Sorry, Mom, I can't. Mounce took my place in this fight, and now he's in trouble.

I managed to sneak up behind Manuello and push him hard enough to knock the inhaler out of his hand. Mounce crawled over to it and sucked in the gas for all he was worth. Manuello turned on me and rained down so many kicks and punches that I was blinded by the pain. Then, suddenly, it stopped. When I opened my eyes again, I saw John sitting on Manuello's chest, giving him a taste of what he just gave me. I pulled Mounce by the arm and we both crawled to the side of the house. I figured we'd wait it out behind these bushes until everybody got tired, or died, or went home. A minute later I heard sirens peeling through the air. The Mexicans jumped into their cars and burned rubber down the street. Georgie and the surfers remained on the lawn, shouting victory whoops as the police cruisers pulled up. Tracy stood in her big picture window, looking like this was the last night of her life.

Half an hour later the only people left were the musicians, who were carring their equipment past Mounce and me out to their truck. We tried to help Tracy pat down the lawn and hide any evidence of the fight. You might have said that we were trying to be noble, but we were stuck there waiting to get picked up by our parents anyway so . . . I slapped Mounce on the back. "You were pretty tough out there, man. Nobody can call you chicken, that's for sure."

Mounce flexed his fists like a prize-fighter. "As long as I can still play the drums."

"Ringo never took a lesson in his life."

"I've had fourteen." We laughed at the joke like two old friends who had survived a war together, and then Mounce's mother drove up. My friend winked at me, brushed himself off one last time, and waved goodnight as he got into his car.

The last of the musicians drove off a minute later and Tracy re-entered her house to finish cleaning up. There was nobody left but me. So I'd been to my first big party, survived my first rumble, and gotten a few scrapes and bruises to brag about which, for the moment, I had neatly hidden under my clothing. All in all, I felt pretty good. In fact, a moment later when my Dad drove up, I was feeling bitchin', that is until Sherry came out of the house. Shit, I forgot all about her. But it all came back to me as we climbed into the back seat of my father's car (careful to hide the cuts and bruises) and sat in stony silence.

"So how was the party, kids?" he asked.

"Good," was all I could manage to say. It wasn't too long before my father picked up on my prickly mood and left us alone which was just as well because if I said anything else, even one more word . . . I glanced over at Sherry sitting there like a perfect little lady.

After what felt like forever we finally arrived at her house and she offered me her prettiest smile. "Well, thanks for a nice night," she said, then she scooted up the walk and disappeared into her house–forever, I hoped.

When we were finally alone, my father turned to me with a big question mark on his face. "Something happened, didn't it? What did I say about treating her like a lady?"

"I treated her like a lady! But she didn't treat *me* like a gentleman!" I couldn't hold back any longer and the tears started streaming down my face as I told him how another guy stole my girl.

"The little bitch!" he cursed as we drove on home.

I guess I hadn't hidden my wounds as well as I thought.

# CHAPTER 25

"I wish I never had to see any of 'em again."

I called Vicki out to show her my Hebrew book and tell her what to expect at my Bar Mitzvah next Saturday, but I really needed to talk to her about last night. She wasn't surprised by any of it–the drinking, the fighting, any of it. Then I told her what I was really worried about which is what Georgie might do to Mounce when he saw him next–and I was a little concerned for myself, too. The thing that I was dreading most was confessing my dirty little scheme to Vicki–trading an invite for Mounce to the party by promising to bring her for Georgie. But amazingly, when I told her, she wasn't even mad.

"Don't sweat it," she said. "I would've done the same thing. Besides, I can handle myself. And if I ever meet up with that little tramp, Sherry, her ass is grass."

This girl amazed me. I told her all about my despicable plan, opened up to her about my fears, even confessed my shame, and what did she do? She tried to make me feel better! Man, this was way different than talking to a guy, even to my best friend, Mounce. It made me feel like I could tell Vicki about anything, even my feelings for her, and I would have, if we weren't interrupted by shouts from down the street.

"Hey, Hombre!" I couldn't believe it! It was Mounce, Georgie, and Eddie stroking up together, thick as thieves.

"Mouncie had to prove himself, didn't ya?" bragged Georgie like old war buddies themselves. "Nobody calls my friend a chicken." Georgie and Mounce slapped each other, showing off for us all.

"I took on Manuello, man!" shouted Mounce.

"And you woulda kicked his ass too if the cops hadn't shown," added Eddie.

Georgie looked at me and then at Vicki and I knew exactly what he was going to say next, but she beat him to the punch. "Sorry about last night," she said coyly. "The audition was way in downtown Hollywood, and you know how the traffic is."

This seemed to sit okay, but you never knew with Georgie. "That girl, Sherry, she's a virgin that needs no urgin', if ya know what I mean. Besides, guys should never let a chick come between 'em, right?" Georgie shoved me and then gestured for me to shove him back. We horsed around a bit to confirm that we were friends again. "So who feels like a little smoke 'n poker?"

Georgie, Eddie, and Mounce charged into my backyard and Vicki and I followed. Five minutes later, we were all sitting in the bamboo thicket, playing cards. Eddie handed me a cigarette. "Don't bogart it." He saw the question mark on my face and explained. "Don't get your lips all over it. We want some too."

I wiped my mouth dry and placed the thin edge of my lips over the cigarette to keep my saliva off the cancer stick. Eddie gave me a queer look. "And you're gonna be a man?" he said.

I hacked out a 'yes' as I gestured to my Hebrew book. "In five days. I sing these prayers, we have a party—which is just for the family (God, I hope Mounce and Vicki didn't let on they were the only friends who had been invited)—and I get presents. I'm hoping for a new guitar."

Georgie grinned over his cards. "Around here, if ya wanna be a man, ya gotta screw a woman, right, Vicki?"

"That's right, then tell everyone you know about it," she quipped.

Everyone laid down their cards. Vicki had the low hand. "Whoops," cackled Georgie. I suddenly remembered someone said something about strip poker, but I figured they were joking, until Eddie hopped behind Vicki and held her arms while Georgie unbuttoned her blouse.

"She said no, Georgie," I shouted.

Off came Vicki's blouse revealing a lacy white bra. "I didn't hear her say anything," he replied.

"Well, I did, and this is my property. You have to go now, everybody. Get off of my property."

"Get off your property?" he barked. "Get out of my country!" Georgie reached around and pulled a knife out of his back pocket. Then he put the blade to my face and traced a line from my cheek to my chin. Mounce tried to lighten things up.

"Georgie, man, come on, he didn't mean nothin'. You said yourself about never letting a chick come between friends, right?"

"Georgie? Gimme a drag?" Vicki purred.

With the knife still on me, Eddie handed a cigarette to Georgie, who took one huge drag, then leaned over and put his mouth on Vicki's. After a few seconds (which felt like forever), he came off her and she exhaled the smoke. That's when I almost grabbed Georgie's knife and stabbed him in the chest before he even knew what happened. I imagined him looking back at me, wide-eyed, as if to say, "Dude, I didn't know you had it in ya."

And I would have too, if it wasn't for my Bubie.

"Sandy? Where's my Sandy?" That ancient European accent could only belong to one person.

"That's my Bubie. My Bubie is here!" I shouted.

"What's a Bubie?" Eddie asked.

The game was over. I stood up now, unafraid as Georgie folded his knife and put it back in his pocket. Vicki did up her blouse and the five of us left the bamboo thicket to find my whole family standing in the backyard with my grandmother, Bubie Diamond – a short, stocky woman with squinting eyes and a perpetual smile. I ran to give her a big hug for saving my life and preventing a possible bloodbath.

"So big and so strong you're getting!" she said.

Mounce, Eddie, and Georgie said their goodbyes as innocently as could be. When Vicki waved to me and crossed to her house, I couldn't even look at her. My parents gave me a "What were you all up to back there?" look, but it was forgotten as Bubie showered us with praises and thanks to God for helping us grow into such beautiful grandchildren in the warm, nurturing, California sun.

Dinner that evening was livelier than it had been in a long time as Bubie gave us a rundown on our relatives back home. Then it was our turn to tell her about our adventures. She sat there listening, amused and amazed, the perfect audience for six homesick souls. Afterwards, we decided to give her a show and dress up in the new suits my parents bought us for the weekend's festivities. I let the younger ones go first and waited down the hall to be last; after all, it was my Bar Mitzvah.

I could overhear my mother nattering away like a magpie. "It's not a big synagogue, Ma, but it's very nice, you know. The food is kosher and you'll love the Rabbi, he's a very nice man and he says Steven has a wonderful voice, the best he's heard from any of his pupils," which floored me because this was the first time either of my parents had acknowledged my music. Maybe this whole Bar Mitzvah thing wasn't going to be so bad after all.

"With such a voice maybe one day he'll grow up to be a cantor. Maybe even a Rabbi, why not?" Bubie added.

I figured at that point I'd better make my entrance before they enrolled me in a rabbinical institute. When I did make my entrance dressed in my new suit, with my kepah and tallis, the look on my Bubie's face gave me a new and unexpected appreciation of what this was really all about–as if I'd grown into something bigger and better than the kid she saw half an hour ago.

"You know how long I've waited for my first grandson to be Bar Mitzvah'd?" she squealed.

"Yeah. Thirteen years, right, Bubie?" cracked Paul. "And I'm next, right?"

Any other time a comment like that from my brother

would have been rewarded with a crack right back from me which would have escalated into a fight my parents would have had to stop on pain of death (probably mine). But tonight I couldn't be angry with Paul or anyone in the world. Tonight I was just happy to be standing in my own living room basking in the love of my family. And I made a promise to myself that everything was going to work out here.

Later that evening, my Dad wandered out into the backyard toward the back fence. I followed him, a little worried he might find the Playboys I'd hidden in the bamboo stalks or somehow uncover some of the things that went on back there earlier.

"Nice having Bubie down here to help celebrate, huh?" I mentioned off-handedly.

"Your mother hasn't been this happy in a long time. I think out of all of us, she's been the most homesick."

"How about you?" I asked.

He was eyeballing the whole area suspiciously. "I'm okay as long as the family is okay . . . hmm, but my pomegranate tree is not doing too well."

"Maybe this climate is no good," I suggested.

"Are you kidding? Fruit like this thrives in California. You know what it is, it's the damn bamboo. The roots spread out under the soil and choke the life out of all the other vegetation around it. That's why you don't see anything else growing in this garden. This patch needs to come out."

"You can't do that, it's my spot," I protested. "You guys have the whole house, and I don't have anything of my own. I even have to share my bedroom with my brother. This is my only place."

Dad played with the dying shrub a minute and then returned to the house without saying a word. Was he really concerned over some little bush or was he suspicious about what had been going on back there earlier with my friends? Hard to tell, my Dad rarely came out and said what was on his mind. Not that I didn't know his moods. I knew that he was slow to anger–and that if we ignored the signs, he'd bop us–no surprises there. Most of the time he was pretty even-keeled. He'd even kid around with us every once in a while. But he was not one of those dads who'd take you out in the backyard and throw a ball with you, or take you to a baseball game or go fishing or anything like that. In fact, I don't think he had a single hobby. He was a good man but not what I'd call affectionate. He kept his distance—like the time he handed me the sex book and then left the room. He just tossed things out there and hoped we'd figure it out for ourselves. I did know that he loved us, and that he worked himself to the bone from early morning to after dark–maybe that was why he had no time for hobbies–and I knew it took a lot of guts for him to move out here to make a better life for us all. Because of that and because I'm the eldest, I owed it to him to help make it work. But beyond that, I actually didn't know very much about the man.

## Today I am a Man

# CHAPTER 26

I to think I had two voices in my head: the one telling me how great I was and that whatever I was thinking at the moment was the best idea in the world, and the other voice telling me that the first voice was only lying to get what it wanted. That second voice was the one I usually ignored until it proved itself right, and then when it did, all I wanted was to kick the shit out of the first voice.

I was at my locker when Eddie jogged over with an extra wide grin on his face. "Hey, Steve!" He handed me a skateboard—a beauty.

"How come?" I asked.

"It's from me and Georgie—a present for your bar thing. We felt bad about yesterday, so . . ."

I didn't know what to say. Georgie must have realized

he went too far. Maybe he wasn't as bad as I thought (that was, of course, the first voice talking).

"Thanks, thanks a lot. Tell Georgie, too." I shoved the board in my locker and worried that maybe the trouble the other day was all my fault. Maybe what happened was that when they heard about my Bar Mitzvah party and found out they weren't invited, they got pissed. Now that I thought about it, they did invite me to Tracy's party, and I started feeling bad about not inviting them to my bar.

Best thing to do was to bounce this off Mounce while we walked to gym class. "Sure they feel bad 'cause they *are* bad. Nobody gives you a skateboard for free."

"Not even if it's a present? By the way . . ." I pulled one of our new band cards out of my pocket, the ones I made in print shop. It read, "The Vulcans – for parties and dances," and this one included Mounce's phone number along with mine. We both agreed the new card was bitchin' and we couldn't wait to start giving them out. As we talked about the new songs we were going to learn and all the band work we were going to get, Mister Hunter caught me in the locker room and told me I was wanted in the V.P.'s office. There was only one reason a kid was sent to see Mr. Cole.

The V.P.'s office was like a police station; not that I've ever actually been in one. When I walked in, the secretary already knew who I was, and gave me a stern look. It was like they finally caught this outlaw and couldn't wait to see him swing for his crimes, whatever they were. She sent me right into Mr. Cole's office and closed the door behind me. There he was sitting behind his desk like a warden, dressed in the same white shirt, dark tie, and navy suit he always wore. Then I realized why I was here–the skateboard Eddie gave me was sitting right there on Mister Cole's desk.

"It was reported stolen; we did a locker check and found it in yours," Cole said, watching for my reaction. In a flash, everything Mounce said about Georgie came back to me. That's when I began listening to that second voice of mine, the one that made me want to kick the shit out of the first voice. I stood there speechless, which by the scowl on his face, was not what Mr. Cole wanted to hear.

"A boy comes into my office, stands slouched in front of me with his hands in his pockets, and doesn't even answer when he's spoken to?"

I took my hands out of my pockets and stood ramrod straight. "I know about the board, Mr. Cole. I mean I put it there. I mean somebody gave it to me so I put it in my locker, sir."

"Somebody who?" he demanded.

I could have told Mr. Cole that it was Eddie Lopez but then I could also have gotten the shit kicked out of me every day for the rest of my life too, or I could keep my mouth shut.

Mr. Cole picked up a manila folder, opened it slowly, and started reading. "Sanford Goldman, transferred from Toronto, Canada, three months ago. No detentions, no prior disciplinary problems . . . until now. Sanford, either you stole another boy's board or you took it knowing full well that no one gets something for nothing. Either way, it's a pretty dumb move, isn't it? Now I want to know who gave you this skateboard."

I stayed silent while commanding every muscle in my body to remain still. To tell the truth, Mr. Cole didn't look surprised. I really don't think he expected me to fink on a friend.

"Five detentions beginning this afternoon after school. Now get out of here," he barked. When I returned to class, Eddie and Georgie were there waiting for me with smirks on their faces.

"It's like a test to see if you rat on your friends or take it like a man," said Georgie.

"Yeah, our version of a Bar Mitzvah," Eddie added. Mounce, who heard it all from a few seats back, just shook his head.

At the end of the day, I made my way to the detention room, cursing myself. If I took the detentions, I'd be the joke of the school for getting conned by Georgie and Eddie. If I didn't take the detentions . . . standing at the door, I thought about what a sucker I had been, then I made my decision and kept walking.

"You're right, Steven, sometimes life is not fair and you need someone on your side. First thing tomorrow morning I am going down to your school to have a man-to-man talk with Mister Cole, and I will make him understand that this was not your fault. Don't worry about a thing." This is what I would have liked my father to have said. Instead, the conversation went more like:

"One week before your Bar Mitzvah and you pull this?"

"I didn't pull anything, I was tricked," I claimed in my own defense.

"By whom?" he demanded.

"I can't tell you."

"Is that what you told the vice principal?"

"You just don't go finking on people in school."

"Then you deserve to be punished. This is stealing!"

"But I didn't steal anything!"

"You can call it anything you want, but the fact is you took something that didn't belong to you and that's stealing. I thought you were smarter than that."

No one made a sound at the dinner table. This was too serious to joke about especially before my Bar Mitzvah, although my brother Paul was silently bursting with joy that it was me who was in trouble and not him. Even the two little ones sensed the sour mood. But the person I felt worst for was my grandmother, who came five thousand miles to see this happen.

"I'm sure Sandy didn't steal," she said. "He's not that kind of boy."

Dad ignored her and made his pronouncement. "You know what? Sometimes life is not fair, so learn a lesson, son: you don't steal and you don't be a patsy for someone who does. And if you do, then you pay the consequences. I think you should tell Mr. Cole who is responsible and don't let yourself be bullied by this guy, whoever he is. That's what a man would do."

Thanks Dad, it's been nice knowing you. I stormed out of the house.

A few minutes later, I was at the convenience store where Georgie and Eddie had brought me a couple of weeks ago. There was nobody in the shop except me and Norm, the manager. I walked down the aisle and picked up a candy bar with my left hand while my right hand stuffed three others down my pants. Then I walked up to Norm and paid him for the candy bar in my hand.

"Not too busy tonight, huh, Norm?" I mention off-handedly.

"Nope, not tonight."

I smiled and he smiled and I walked out the door. A minute later, at the edge of the parking lot, I pulled out my stash. Took 'em right from under his nose. Am I good or what? I am fucking good. I am bitchin'! But that bitchin' feeling didn't last very long.

The next day in English class, my mind wandered ahead to Saturday morning where I saw myself reciting my prayers as my proud parents sat with the congregation, admiring their son, the candy thief. Then the walls of the synagogue fell away and I found myself in a cell surrounded by bars and my new blue suit transformed into a striped prison uniform. Thankfully, the trance was broken when I heard someone calling my name. Thankfully, that is, until I recognized the voice and looked up to see Mister Cole's hulking frame in the doorway.

"Sandford Goldman," repeated the Voice of Doom.

Mine was the last name anyone expected to hear coming out of Mister Cole's mouth and everyone in class, including Mrs. Clarke, looked at me with surprise, everyone except Georgie and Eddie. Mounce gave me a look that told me that he felt my pain. I had no choice but to get up and follow Mr. Cole out the door.

No one walked these halls between classes except the honor students who acted more like prison guards. When I passed one of them on my way to Cole's office, he stared at me like I was a convicted criminal on my way to the gas chamber. Maybe my daydream was actually coming true. Was it too late to take the candy bars back?

"Take everything out of your pockets and place them on the desk," commanded the V.P. Mounce told me he never saw it coming, but I did. It was a large, red paddle sitting right there on his desk. I pulled out my comb and some loose change and lay them on the desk, careful not to let my hands shake. "You never reported for your detentions, Sandford."

"My name is Steven." Correcting him about my name was my only form of protest.

"Grab your ankles, Steven," he ordered.

I bent over and took a few shallow breaths. My mission was to get through this without showing any tears or fears, because at Christopher Columbus Junior High School, that's what it was to be a man. I could feel him watching me, sizing me up before he administered the hurt he was about to inflict. Foolishly, I was hoping that the anticipation would be worse than the actual pain itself. I clenched my buttocks to minimize the sting but I could only hold it for so long and as soon as I let go, whack!–the paddle found its mark. I winced and let go of my ankles. Not so bad. No tears at least.

"Did I tell you to stand up?" he said. Over I went again, grabbing my ankles. I clenched and waited.

"This country has been called a great melting pot,

Steven. It accepts people from all over the world and has a lot to offer but in return it asks something from each of us. It asks us to follow the rules." Whack! Did he actually hit me harder this time or did it just feel that way? While I was thinking about that, he let go with a third. Jesus Christ!

"You can stand up now and put your things back in your pocket," said the bastard. I took my comb and change off his desk, careful not to let him see how much this hurt me, but I could not stop the trembling of my hands.

"Now I don't want to see you in my office again. Understand?" If I opened my mouth even to say "Yessir," I knew I would lose it, so I just nodded and left. On the way back to class, the image of that great melting pot came to mind, and I stuffed Georgie, Eddie, and Mr. Cole into it and watched them all boil to death.

Seeing as it was almost the end of the school day, I figured I'd grab my things from my locker and go home. At this point, I almost dared anyone to report me for leaving early and if they did, I told myself I would never take another swat again even if it meant that they'd expel me. Trudging home through the fields, I imagined a dozen other ways to kill Georgie, Eddie, and Mr. Cole. When I got bored with that, I imagined that Cole went too far with his punishment and sent me to the hospital, where my parents waited anxiously in the emergency room as I hovered near death and they cursed themselves for allowing this to happen to their favorite son. By the time I actually did get home I felt much better, mostly because I had now plotted out how to get my revenge. I'd decided to write down every single detail of my trip to Mr. Cole's office and use it as my Bar Mitzvah speech to recite in front of the whole congregation and humiliate my parents. Somebody must pay! But when I got home, I realized that a few lousy swats were the least of my problems.

# CHAPTER 27

"Mom?"

"She's not here, Steven."

Was that Vicki's voice I heard in the other room? When I got to the den I found her sitting there with Paul, Dustin, and Honey. I hadn't said a word to her since the other day in the bamboo thicket, and I was sure as hell not going to speak to her now.

"What is *she* doing here?" I asked Paul.

"Bubie wasn't feeling so hot so Mom took her to the doctor. Vicki's here to babysit the kids."

Fine! I wheeled around and headed off to my room, slamming the door, and pounded away on my guitar. Who needed Vicki? Who needed my parents? Who needed anyone? Then the door opened, and there she was holding my baby sister in her arms.

"I'm practicing!" I growled–not that that had stopped her before. She came in and just stood there, waiting, until I couldn't stand it anymore. "Didn't you hear me? I said, get out!"

"I know you're pissed; you wanna talk about it?" she asked softly.

Why the hell would I want to talk about it? I did what my father did when he had a fight with my mother which was to give her the silent treatment. "Gimme my sister!"

I took Honey from Vicki and sat on the floor. Honey was the only girl who accepted me as I was and asked nothing from me. All she wanted was to roll around and play, which was fine with me because it was the perfect way to ignore Vicki, who still hadn't taken the hint and left. Didn't she know how much she hurt me the other day? Didn't she know how much it hurt being in the same room with her? I wanted to get back at her so bad, hurt her as much as she hurt me, but what could I do, punch her in the arm? Dealing with a girl was such a pain! The only thing I knew was what I had learned from my father, which was to shut down totally in silence. This made my mother stew until the poison built up inside her and she couldn't take it anymore–and exploded. Sounded good to me until I couldn't stand it any more and I was the one who exploded.

"Alright, you wanna know why I'm pissed off? I'll tell you why: you let Eddie take off your shirt and then you let Georgie kiss you!"

"He had a knife on you, what was I supposed to do?" replied Vicki.

"You think I need you to protect me? I'm not a kid,"

"I know, I'm sorry." My baby sister's bottom lip started to quiver as she picked up on my anger, so for her sake I changed the subject and lowered my voice.

"Got a swat today. Three of 'em. Didn't hurt."

"Old man Cole, huh? Tell me what happened. Tell me everything." She asked in such a sweet, sympathetic voice that it all poured out of me — how Eddie set me up with the skateboard and every detail that led up to the swats. After I unloaded, Vicki sat down beside me, very still. We watched Honey play on the floor a minute, and then Vicki leaned in and kissed me on the cheek. Like magic, the poison in my stomach disappeared but now I was bothered by a different feeling. What was that kiss for exactly? Did she feel sorry for me or was she trying to make up for kissing Georgie? Did she want me to kiss her back and if I did, should I kiss her on the cheek or on the lips? I never got the chance to find out because my brother Paul burst into my room, his face as white as a ghost.

"Bubie's dead!"

A minute later my Dad appeared at the door looking

tired and pale. "Your grandmother passed away today. It was a heart attack. Your Mom is still at the hospital."

It was late when my mother finally got home that night, almost eleven-thirty. Vicki had left and the other kids had gone to bed but I told my Dad that I would wait up for Mom no matter what time she came in. She sat down at the kitchen table, her face looking drawn and worn out from crying. She wasn't a big woman, but tonight she looked especially small, tiny even. I gave her a hug and felt her using me to draw strength before she gathered her thoughts.

"Dad had a talk with the Rabbi. He said there's nothing in Jewish law that says we can't go ahead with your Bar Mitzvah this Saturday if we want to. But I need to take my mother back home and I can't send her on a plane by herself, do you understand?"

I nodded, trying to understand.

"When I return to Toronto I will have to make arrangements for the funeral and say Kaddish . . . I'll be gone for a few weeks. Steven, I know how hard you've worked on your haftorah reading, and I know how long you've looked forward to this day, but I want you to know we are not canceling your Bar Mitzvah, we are only postponing it."

There was no way this was fair or right to ask of me, but there was also no way I could say no. She held my face in her hands and kissed me and then I watched her make tearful phone calls to my aunts and uncles back in Toronto. After a while, when I couldn't stand to hear her weep anymore, I went to bed. Sometimes you drift off to sleep, sometimes you fall asleep. That night I dropped like a rock into a deep, dark pool.

Today I am a Man

# CHAPTER 28

Next morning, Mounce and I had a lot to talk about: my grandmother dying, my Bar Mitzvah being postponed. He told me he had lost both his grandparents, so he knew how I felt. When we got around to what happened in Cole's office, he already knew–news like that travels fast in school. But the good thing was that because I didn't rat out Georgie and Eddie and took my punishment like a man, I passed their stupid test so I was cool again. There were all kinds of tests I was being faced with these days. Some I realized I'd pass, some I wouldn't.

Three weeks later, Mom returned from Canada. She put on a happy face as she gave us all an update on everyone back home and before I knew it, my parents were back at the kitchen table making plans for my new Bar Mitzvah. They pretended things were back to normal, but the lie was as obvious as that little bottle of pills my Mom now kept with her for her nerves.

Then as if things weren't complicated enough, the Rabbi explained that each haftorah or set of prayers coincided with a passage in the Torah which is read every week in synagogue. Since we were re-scheduling mine for a few months down the road, the haftorah portion I had memorized *perfectly* could not be used and I'd need to learn an entirely new one. I could whine all I wanted but it wouldn't change a thing. In fact, all it would do would be to make my folks feel worse, as if they didn't have enough on their minds with the money they'd lost on the invitations and the food and the entertainment from the first cancelled event. I told myself this was just another test and if I could endure those swats from Cole, I could endure anything. When I came home, my parents sat me down for another talk. Not more bad news? How much can a thirteen year-old take? Mom, pass me a couple of those pills before you drop the next bombshell.

"You never knew my father, your Zaidy," said Mom. "He was a musician. Every Sunday he'd play his violin on the front porch. The neighbors would come around and pretty soon everybody would be in our house singing and dancing and laughing."

"That's how I met your mother," Dad remarked.

Mom reached up into the cupboard and handed me an envelope filled with a huge wad of cash. "I think it would make both your grandparents very happy if you put this money toward your music," said my mother, beaming.

"At least Bubie got to see me in my suit and tallis," I murmured.

"Yes she did, and that made her very proud," my mother said with a hug.

Was it a coincidence, I wondered, that as soon as I'd accepted my fate of having to learn a new Bar Mitzvah portion, I was rewarded with my grandparent's money to buy the guitar I'd always wanted? Was this the universe telling me that there is a certain balance or justice, if you sacrifice here, you'll receive there? As I sat at the kitchen table counting and recounting the cash, I realized that the tone in the conversation between my parents and I sounded different than in any we'd had before. It wasn't so much 'parent to child' but more 'person to person.' And by giving me this money for my music, they'd acknowledged that I was not just their kid who went to school, ate their food, and slept in their house, but that I was my own person with my own dreams. That they finally got that, amazed me. Maybe I wasn't the only one maturing here!

The following Saturday, we drove to the music shop.

I'd been here hundreds of times with Mounce when he took his drum lessons. I liked to check out all the equipment, especially the electric guitars hanging on the pegboard behind the cash register. Then after his lesson, we'd both listen to the older kids trying out instruments and dreamt that one day we'd be as good as them. In the process, I had picked out the guitar for me.

"That one, Dad." I pointed to a thin, silver, electric with double pick-ups hanging on the board behind the sales desk. The salesman who knew me smiled and lifted it down.

"She's a beauty, isn't she?" he said. "The neck is as straight as an arrow, the frets sit nice and low to give it great action . . . and two pick-ups instead of one."

I strapped the guitar around my shoulder and strummed it. It was like she was made for me and me alone. I was in heaven until my father noticed, "Are those cracks in the wood?" He pointed to the neck, under the strings and sure enough the wood seemed to have tiny cracks in it. I'd never seen them before, I guess because the guitar was hung so high up on the wall. My heart sank and my dreams were dashed against the rocks, but Dad casted his eye around and gestured to another guitar in the same price range. "What about that one?" he asked.

It was a brown mahogany with a sunburst splash across the body. The salesman brought it down and we inspected it all the way from the top peg to the strap clip on the bottom of the body. It wasn't as glittery as the silver one but there were no flaws.

"Since you're almost a regular here, Steven, we'll throw in the strap and one free lesson as part of the deal. Oh, and this being an electric, you'll need an amplifier."

After we left the shop with my new gear, I couldn't help but think that the silver guitar reminded me a lot of L.A. From a distance, it looked amazing until you looked a little closer and noticed the flaws.

When we returned home we found the family waiting for us, anxious to see what I'd bought. We all went out to the backyard where I plugged my new guitar into my new amp, and start playing. Soon my brothers and sister were dancing around like Mexican jumping beans and my parents were shaking their hips to the music. Even a few of the neighbors popped their heads over the fence to listen. This is how it must have been years ago when my grandfather played his fiddle for the neighborhood, when my parents first met. I don't know how, but the moment you strum that new guitar or whack that new cymbal, the music transports you to another place. I was hooked and all I could think of was, wouldn't this sound better with a larger amp or playing with a band or singing with a real microphone and mike stand? More, bigger, better. It is a sickness, ask any musician.

Mounce's parents bought him another drum and a new cymbal for his birthday and pretty soon we were sounding pretty good, even getting some gigs. Our first one was a backyard birthday party. I saved up for a microphone but I couldn't afford the stand so I had to wrap the cord around the branch of a tree and sing into it, which worked alright except for the sore neck I had afterwards. Somebody at the party liked us and asked us to play for their party. This time there was no tree in the yard so I had to lay my mike down on a picnic table and sing sideways into it. More sore neck. But with the money we made, I could afford to buy my first mike stand. We were even getting known around school and it wasn't long before we got our first big break–from guess who?

"Hear your band is sounding bitchin' these days," said Georgie sitting on top of the monkey bars. "Think you're ready for the big time? The school dance?"

There was only one more school dance before summer holidays and it would normally have gone to The Skaggs, but if anyone could make this happen, it was Georgie. But before I could even think about it, Mounce shouted, "Absolutely!"

Georgie nodded to us as if it was in the bag. Then he added, "Midnight run, Sunday night."

This must be how a mouse feels when he sees that piece of cheese laying there out in the open. He's so hungry for that cheese that he ignores the trap it's sitting in. I told Mounce what I was thinking but he thought I was nuts.

"Georgie's gonna give us our big break and you're scared to go out with him? What are you, stupid?" I was not stupid. I knew that if we didn't go out with him we wouldn't get the gig, but I also knew that if we were good, if we were talented, there'd be other chances. Still, Mounce was determined to play this dance and reminded me how nice Georgie had been to us these past few weeks because I took the swats like a man. He really believed that this was Georgie's way of making up. Maybe I was just a mouse who smelled a rat that wasn't there. After a while I gave in. "Don't worry, I'll protect ya," Mounce joked, hugging me.

"Get off me, ya homo!"

## Today I am a Man

# CHAPTER 29

It was Sunday night and I was in bed watching the clock on my night table as it ticked down to 12:00. I turned to make sure my brother was asleep and, like the last time, gently pulled off my covers and crept out of bed. Already dressed, I shoved two pillows under my sheets as usual and put on my housecoat just in case my parents were still wandering around. All was clear as I tip-toed from my bedroom to the bathroom and closed the door silently behind me. What was I worried about? I'd done this before, but I was feeling edgy. I shoved my bathrobe under the sink and took out the sneakers I hid there earlier, climbed out the window and jogged to the front of my house . . . where I was tackled from behind.

"Jesus, Mounce!" I shouted.

We both trotted down the street a ways and waited at the corner. Mounce was all hopped up about this, and the way he talked made me feel even more nervous.

"My dad's getting me a new standing tom for my drum kit, I beat the shit out of my old one . . . you know, Diane Bannister, the blonde with the big ones? She shoved 'em right in my face yesterday while I was getting up from my seat in the cafeteria, she wants it . . . I heard Bruce from the Skaggs is so pissed 'cause we're going to be playing the last dance . . . he's jealous because I'm a better drummer than him . . ."

Thankfully a minute later two cigarette butts approached us in the dark—Georgie and Eddie—carrying paper bags as usual. Having done this before, I could pretty much figure what pranks they were up to, so this time I set the rules.

"No matches, no lighting toilet paper, or I'm going home,"

"Don't sweat it. That was just your initiation," answered Georgie. "We're not lighting any toilet paper, promise."

"Then what's in the bag?"

Without answering, Georgie and Eddie started off down the street. Mounce nudged me in the ribs to just be cool and follow.

"I'm taking karate lessons in the fall . . ." announced Mounce, "a graduation present from my folks."

Georgie snorted at the idea. "The last thing my old man would give me is karate lessons 'cause he knows I'd use it on him."

"You'd take on your own Dad?" I asked.

"Already did . . ." boasted Eddie, ". . . and kicked his ass for leaving Georgie's Mom for some twenty year-old chick."

Georgie smacked Eddie in the arm to shut him up and then added. "Everybody takes on their old man sooner or later, if you ever wanna grow up."

We stopped on a corner as Georgie looked over a house across the street. Eddie whispered to him, something about this being the one, and Georgie barked, "Woof." Then we all peeled over to the house. Georgie handed out rolls of toilet paper and Mounce and I got busy decorating. Meanwhile, Eddie gathered an armful of circulars and piled them on the doorstep.

When we put on the finishing touches, Georgie pulled me off to the side. "I want you to call Vicki and tell her to meet me tomorrow night."

That's when I understood why he asked us out tonight and why we're getting the dance gig, but I was done being his go'fer. "Look Georgie, if you want to ask her out, why don't you call her yourself?"

"I would, but her old man doesn't like me. Dunno

why. Hey, don't worry, I'll play it safe." And to prove it he pulled his wallet out of his pocket and showed me a condom wrapper. Before I could shove the rubber down his big fat mouth and choke him with it, Eddie ran past us laughing.

"What?" I shouted.

"Cherry bomb!" cackled Georgie as he and Mounce followed Eddie down the street.

"What's a cherry bomb?"

The answer exploded in my ears like a canon. The three delinquents were halfway down the block while I stood there staring stupidly at the burning newspapers on the porch where Eddie had hidden the bomb. The smart thing for me to do would have been to get the hell out of there, so why did I do the exact opposite and race over to stamp out the flames? Bad idea, because a minute later the homeowner whipped open the door to get the surprise of his life, and so did I. I was expecting, at worst, to see some sleepy-eyed accountant in his underwear but instead I was face to face with some big old Hell's Angels dude. In the blink of an eye he had me in a headlock and I was promising God that not only would I be a good boy from now on, but I'd even look into that Rabbinical school if He'd only stop this guy from ripping my head off my shoulders. I guess God must've hated the Hell's Angel more than me, because the miracle happened—the flames singed his bare feet and I wriggled free.

I raced down the block where my future cell mates were hiding behind bushes, laughing at the homeowner who was using his shirt to swat out the flaming newspapers.

"Are you guys crazy? You promised, no fires!"

"No *toilet paper* fires," Eddie said, correcting me.

But Georgie was not even listening. He'd realized that his wallet was missing. "Shit! Probably fell out of my pocket back there when I showed you the safe, Goldman. It's your fault, go get it,"

I pretended not to hear him but Mounce elbowed me in the ribs as if to say, "get the wallet or forfeit the band gig." At that moment two images were fighting for supremacy in my head; playing the school dance against doing the hora in the prison yard in Alcatraz.

"Get it yourself," I offered.

"You little chickenshit!" Georgie hissed like a snake.

"Maybe you're the chickenshit," I replied, "'cause I don't see *you* going back for it."

But before I finished telling Georgie off, Mounce had started making his way back to the house on hands and knees like G.I. Joe.

"Decent, man," said Eddie.

I looked up the street to notice that the homeowner had doused the fire on his porch and gone back inside. Meanwhile Mounce crept up to the lawn and actually found the friggin' wallet, holding it high for everyone to see. That's when the side gate opened and the dude introduced Mounce to his German Shepherd.

"Hi, son, meet Lady," he said with a nasty smile.

And that's when I overheard Eddie say to Georgie, "There she is, just like you said."

The shepherd snarled at Mounce, who just about wet his pants before he turned and ran while Georgie and Eddie howled with laughter. The homeowner stood there with his dog and I hoped to God it was just a scare tactic. When Mounce flew past us, Georgie called out, "Wallet!"

Mounce tossed the wallet to him and kept on running. But when I looked back I realized why the homeowner hadn't moved; he was waiting to find out where the rest of us were hiding before he set the dog loose.

"Go for a fence!" shouted Eddie as all three of us raced down the sidewalk. Georgie spotted a tall fence first and we all hopped it, racing from one back yard to the next, putting distance between us, the dog, and Mounce, who must have taken another route.

Twenty minutes later we made it back to my house, huffing and puffing. Mounce was nowhere in sight. For the first time, Eddie looked nervous, but it wasn't Mounce's safety he was worried about.

"If he gets caught and squeals, I'll kick his fuckin'

ass," he warned.

I turned on both of them. "You guys knew about the dog, didn't you! That's why you picked that house. You set us up! Don't you know Mounce has asthma?"

"Shaddup, cry-baby," Georgie smirked. "He's probably home in bed right now, laughing it off. You say anything about tonight and you're a dead man, you hear?"

As the two of them shuffled off, Eddie turned back with a parting shot. "If he does show, you tell him we said he's a man–not a baby like you." Georgie lit another cigarette and soon they were both just a couple of butts glowing in the night.

There was nothing for me to do now but wait. Part of me hoped Mounce would at any minute come jogging down the street; the other part hoped he was home in bed laughing his head off, which would be fine with me, too. I just wanted to know one way or the other that he was okay but it wasn't like I was going to call his house and ask his parents to check if he was in bed. After a few minutes, I gave up and headed back to the side of my house, hoping it would all sort itself out in the morning. But just as I boosted myself up through the window the light in the bathroom went on and I had to jump back down. Just what I needed–to get caught on a night like this. Whoever was in there peed, flushed, and left . . . or maybe they saw me and it was a trap. Tonight anything could happen. I held my breath and counted to 60 before I popped my head back up again; thank God, no one was there. But what if I opened the bathroom door and they were waiting for me in the hall? I was so racked with guilt and worry that I almost wished my parents would catch me so I could tell them about this whole crazy night. Almost. I opened the door. No one was there. I breathed a sigh of relief, crept into my room, and climbed under the covers. Home free, I thought, until I heard. . . . "Where were you?" It was the voice of my brother Paul in the other bed.

"In the bathroom."

"No you weren't. You haven't been in bed for awhile."

"You were *dreaming* that I haven't been in bed for awhile and you're still dreaming now. Go back to sleep," I said, turning over.

# CHAPTER 30

First thing next morning, I called Mounce, but nobody answered at his house so I figured he'd already left for school, but when I got there he wasn't in class. Georgie and Eddie cornered me to ask if I knew anything, so obviously they hadn't seen him either. After lunch, rumors started floating around that soeone had heard a couple of teachers talking about a kid who got attacked by a dog last night. The rumors got bigger and nuttier until the story went that three kids got bitten by a rabid dog and they all had to go to the hospital to get rabies shots where you get a series of needles in the stomach that hurt like hell. I asked Mrs. Clarke if she knew anything, but she told me to pay no mind to rumors. As the day dragged on, Georgie and Eddie lost their smirks. Were they worried about Mounce, or were they worried about Mounce ratting on them? It turned out they had nothing to worry about.

In class, Mounce and I had been forced to read "The Pit In The Pendulum," The Tell-Tale Heart," and "The Fall Of The House Of Usher," all stories written by Edgar Allen Poe that we ended up falling in love with. We even got to see some of them when they were turned into movies starring Vincent Price. This day started out just like one of those horror stories that began in a funeral parlor with heavy drapes and people sitting in pews, mourning. The mood was not so much evil as somber. The air seemed to be making people ill, or maybe everyone looked ill because of why they were there.

Mounce, or Ricky Mountjoy, as they refered to him that day, had a big family that took up the entire first three rows. I could see his pretty mother sitting up there at the front with her husband, whom I had never met before. There were also older brothers, a sister, aunts and uncles, filling the seats. My parents asked me if I wanted to go up to Mounce's folks and give them my condolences, but I couldn't. They said they understood, but they didn't, and I wasn't going to explain it right now. Mounce's casket rested at the front of the room and people were lining up in front of it for the viewing. Some of them were students who waved me over. They knew Mounce and I were best friends, so when I went up they let me ahead of them. I tried to go, but each time was afraid because I knew he was there waiting for me. My stomach was tied in knots when

I finally took those last awful steps. When I got there, my worst fears came true: Mounce's eyes suddenly flew open and he screamed at me, "Why'd you leave me with that dog, asshole? What kind of friend are you?"

"I warned you not to go on that run, didn't I?" I replied helplessly. "You always told me I didn't know who I was dealing with, and what did you do? All for the sake of a gig? It wasn't enough we tried to burn a guy's house down, but you had to show Georgie what a big man you were by going back for his fuckin' wallet. *His* fuckin' wallet, man, not yours! Don't look at me like that, this isn't my fault . . . where the hell did you go, anyway, why didn't you follow us? If you had, you'd have been in class instead of in a fuckin' coffin. And what am I supposed to do now? My best friend dead, and I'm stuck going to his funeral, the first one in my life, and having to deal with the mess left behind. It might not be fair to you, but it's sure as shit not fair to me either! And you know what else . . . you know what else?

I returned to sit with my parents and wait for the service to begin. Glancing around I saw Eddie with some other kids. But I didn't see Georgie.

When everyone who wanted to visit Mounce a final time were done, the Minister addressed the audience in a strong, and powerful voice. Don't ask me what he said, because I was too busy apologizing to Mounce for what I had just said to him in my mind. After the service, my folks suggested we not go to the cemetery, which was fine with me. I couldn't watch them lower my best friend into some dirty grave anyway. I was about ready to leave when Eddie took me aside.

"Listen: you, me, and Georgie, we gotta stick together on this, right? Keep quiet about what happened, right? Surf rules." I could not look at Eddie without wanting to smash his face in, so I just walked away and joined my parents without saying a word. I'd said too much already.

# CHAPTER 31

It turned out that making midnight runs and T.P.'ing homes was a popular sport in the Valley. The police didn't generally make a big deal of it, but Mounce's death took it way beyond and they mounted a whole investigation. A few days later, our class even got a visit from two police officers who told us that Mounce died not of a dog bite like the rumor went, but from a lack of oxygen. What they meant was that he died from an asthma attack while he was being chased by the dog. They also knew he wasn't alone, and we were told that if anyone knew anything, it was their responsibility as a friend of Mounce to tell the school authorities or the police who was there that night.

After class, Georgie and Eddie gave me a lecture about how the cops were the enemy and that none of us would get into any trouble so long as we all kept our mouths shut. Besides, they said, it was the dog owner who was really responsible for killing Mounce, not us. I wasn't so sure.

Keeping our mouths shut didn't make things go away, and about a week later, there was a knock on our door at home. When I opened it up to find Mister and Mrs. Mountjoy, sweat started dripping from the nape of my neck all the way down to my underwear. My folks invited them into the den and sent the other kids out so we adults could talk.

"Steven, we know you and Ricky were great friends, you had so much in common," said Mrs. Mountjoy in a warm but broken voice. "We gave Ricky drum lessons for his birthday a couple of years ago, but he never took them seriously until you two started that band of yours; what did you call yourselves?"

"The Vulcans," I answered meekly. "Mounce, uh, Ricky came up with the name."

Mister Mountjoy took it from there. "Ricky was our youngest child, Steve, our baby, and since you two were so close, we were hoping that . . . we only know a few things about that night. We do know that he was running with some bad kids who T.P.'ed a neighborhood house and set some newspapers on fire. That's when things got out of hand. The homeowner's dog got loose and went after the kids but it was Ricky who was attacked. As you know he had asthma . . . and his heart gave out. But why he was there in the first place, who he was with . . . Steven, were you there with him that night?

"No. I was home sleeping," I waited to see if God would strike me down with lightning. In the meantime, I tried not to look at my parents, who were horrified by what they were hearing. Thank God Paul was in the other room.

Mrs. Mountjoy continued. "We don't want to punish anyone but if you know anything or hear anything from your friends, it's important to tell us. It's important to Ricky's memory, you understand?"

I nodded as if I did.

The Mountjoys got up, and my mother walked them to the door while I stood there with a look on my face that everyone took for grief but was more about wondering if I had really gotten away with the lie. I honestly could not believe that nobody saw through me. I mean, I was just a kid and they were adults. Was I that good a liar, and if I was, how long could I keep it up? God only knew, or maybe I fooled him, too.

There was only one person I could talk to about this: Vicki.

"If you admit to anything," she warned, "do you think they're just going to say, 'Gee thanks Steven,' and leave you alone? Mounce's old man is a lawyer, for Christ sakes. He'll have to call in the police and you could be an accessory to murder. And what about the homeowner, Mister Hell's Angel?

What if he decides to put a contract out on you? There's nothing you can do to help Mounce now anyway, so I think this time Georgie and Eddie are right. For your own protection, just keep quiet."

I wanted to believe Vicki, but this lie was like a festering sore that wouldn't go away. Besides the torture of weighing what I should do against the trouble I'd get into for doing it, there was the constant, nagging problem of dealing with Georgie and Eddie every damn day. I still hadn't promised them I'd keep my mouth shut, so it was open season on guess who. Whenever they caught me in the halls, they'd body-check me into a locker or trip me or spit in the water fountain before I took a drink. One day in class, Georgie leaned over and whispered, "Hey Goldfinger, I saw Mounce's ghost in the head before class. Pissed all over him." I grabbed the nearest book and threw it at him.

The next thing I knew I was back in Mr. Cole's office.

"How did it start? What did he say? Grab your ankles," he commanded.

Not this time. I'd taken enough of his shit and when Cole reached for the paddle on the desk I beat him to it and whacked him on the hands. Then when he went for the door to get help, I booted his ass into the corridor, sending him head-first into a bunch of students who turned and applauded me. Then Eddie came tearing around the corner and I whacked him with the paddle before he even knew what hit him. It sent him flying into the opposite wall and turned his sly grin into a streaky, bloody pulp. While I stood there watching Eddie bleed out on the floor, Georgie sneaked up and blind-sided me with a kick to my ribs. Down on my knees, I waited as he prepared to finish me off with a lethal judo chop, that is until Mounce stayed his arm and plowed him in the face, dropping him like the sack of shit he was. Having recovered, I picked Georgie up, dusted him off, and slugged him in the face, sending him over to Mounce who returned the favor. We continued our little game until Georgie finally collapsed and the entire student body went wild cheering us! Then Mounce and I hugged each other and . . . WHACK! Mr. Cole's paddle brought me back to the real world.

I thought the violence I had to endure was only limited to our school, but it was spreading like a disease everywhere these days, even into a little place in downtown L.A. called Watts. The newspapers said it all started when a white cop pulled over a black man in his own neighborhood and arrested him just because he looked suspicious. Before anyone knew it, all the negroes were rioting, tearing down their own homes and businesses. White people were being told to stay out of Watts but everybody said this was just the beginning. People were afraid they were going to try and take over the city, the country, even. One of our neighbors showed me a rifle he bought which he kept in his truck and told me he had lots of friends who were doing the same. This guy said we all might be forced out of our homes and have to hide up in the mountains until we were strong enough to take the U.S. back again. This sounded as crazy as when we'd sit under our desks during those air raid drills back in Toronto, talking about the end of civilization, only now I wasn't thinking so much about re-populating the world as getting out of the current situation alive.

People said the riots were occurring because life was not fair, and they were right. It wasn't not fair that black people got arrested for driving around in their own neighborhood. It wasn't fair that I got a swat because Eddie gave me a stolen skateboard. It wasn't fair that I had to learn a whole new Bar Mitzvah portion after I had so perfectly memorized my first one. And it wasn't fair that Mounce had to die at the age of thirteen because he was bullied into going back for Georgie's wallet.

# CHAPTER 32

I didn't go out very much after that. I had homework and my new haftorah portion to study, but it was hard to concentrate on either of them. We were discussing the domino effect in social studies class, how one thing happens to affect the next thing down the line and so forth, and I tried to think back to the first domino that tipped over and led to Mounce's death. I wondered if that was that same domino that pushed its brothers one by one out of the San Fernando Valley and into Watts, and from there, all the way around the world to Vietnam. Or had the violence started there and made its way here? I also worried about where I stood in the path of those dominos; was I at the end of the line, or somewhere in the middle, or had I started the whole thing in the first place by moving to L.A., which made me responsible for killing my best friend! Maybe if we never started the band or Mounce hadn't showed me to my class that first day . . . while I was staring at my lessons and wondering where and when this was all going to end, my Mom called me to the front door. Who now? Mounce's parents again? The police? The FBI? It was Georgie and Eddie, looking sorrier than I'd never seen them.

"Can we talk?" asked Georgie.

I wanted to slam the door in both their faces but what if that was a mistake? What if they finally understood what they had been doing was wrong, and I could find a way to stop those dominos from crashing down on me and my family? I stepped outside and closed the door so no one would hear. Then Eddie stepped up quietly.

"We just wanna say this . . ." and he socked me in the jaw. I turned away stunned more than hurt, until Georgie hit me, too, making me drop my Hebrew book on the porch.

"That's nothing compared to what we'll do if you talk, Jew-boy." I watched them turn and walk away, picked up my book and re-entered my house, hurrying back to my room. My father caught me in the hallway.

"That was nice of your friends to drop by. What did they want?"

I couldn't hold back any longer. "What's wrong with me? I dress like them, I talk like them! I'm not black or brown. I look just like them. So why don't they like me? I wish you never brought us here!"

I ran into my room and slammed the door. Maybe there were no answers. Even if I promised Georgie I'd keep my mouth shut, we still wouldn't be friends because Alfredo was right, I didn't belong here, and they didn't want me here.

I overheard my parents in their room whispering. "He spends too much time in his room, and when he's not, you can't talk to him."

"It's hard losing a friend at his age. Give him time," Mom answered as she popped another pill, then added, "Maybe he's right. Maybe we *should* think about going home. We were going to return anyway if he got called up in the draft."

"This is our home," barked my father. "Besides, you know I can't! How could we go back with all the money I owe back there?"

That was when it hit me like a shovel in the back of the head; my father didn't move here because of the weather or because he wanted to give us a better life. He was running away from money problems! And if we went back home now and he got in trouble, that, too, would be all my fault.

A few minutes later Mom came into my room carrying a load of laundry and began separating my clothes from my brother's. She was a smart one to corner me here in my own room. I couldn't even tell her to leave because she was doing something nice for me. Very sneaky.

"Look, I don't know what the trouble is you're having with these boys, " she said, "but I don't think it's so much about how you dress or how you look. If there's some kind of misunderstanding, the only way to clear things up is by talking."

Of course, in a way, she was right. I never actually promised Georgie that I would keep my mouth shut about that night. Maybe if I talked it would solve my problems, and not just mine but Dad's, too. All of ours. When I thought about it, it might be the solution to everything; I fix my problem here and then everything quiets down in Watts, and then the war in Vietnam ends and the draft is over. What if I could stop all the dominos from falling?

Then my mother asked, "Steve, does this have anything to do with your friend, Mounce?" I shook my head, no–what's another lie if it ultimately brought world peace? But damn, how had she gotten so close to the truth?

The next day, I walked over to Georgie's place. I'd never actually been there before and when I saw it, I felt sad for him. The house needed a new paint job, the lawn needed to be mowed and the bushes needed a trimming. I knew about his father who ran out on him and there was talk of a brother who got married and moved away, so I could imagine how hard it must have been for Georgie being the only man in the house at his age. The front door was open, but the screen door in front of it was locked. I'd pretty well rehearsed what I was going to say. It wasn't much, but maybe simple was best. I could hear a few boys inside joking around but as soon as I knocked, everything went quiet. A minute later Eddie came down the hall to the front door.

"Hey Eddie. Is Georgie here? I want to talk . . ." Eddie's foot came flying right through the screen, kicking me in the stomach, and sending me back into the bushes.

"Don't come 'round here no more, Jew-boy. Bad enough we gotta see you at school." He slammed the door as I lay there on the ground, trying to catch my breath. So much for world peace.

My folks noticed me becoming even more moody than usual. The little ones knew it, too, and avoided me when they could. Even my brother Paul steered clear of anything that might start a fight. One night we turned out the lights for bed. Neither of us could sleep, and after a while Paul couldn't keep quiet anymore. "It's going around how Georgie and Eddie are picking on you."

I laid there silently in the dark while he tried again: "The night Mounce died, I heard you sneak out."

Shit! All I needed was for the little prick to try to blackmail me. "It's none of your damn business, you hear? You say anything and you're a dead man! What's your favorite way to die, because I'll make sure that's the one I don't use."

"I wasn't going to tell on you," Paul said, "I was just saying that I know what's bugging you."

This is not what I expected. Before, whenever my brother got something juicy on me he'd use it to hurt, bribe or blackmail me. This time I could hear in his voice that he was not angling for anything and I softened up a bit. "Look, Paul, we can't say anything because if we do, it'll ruin it for the whole family, understand? It's my problem and I've got to fix it."

"How?" he asked.

I gave him the only answer I could: "I dunno."

It wasn't much of a conversation, but for the first time I sensed that he was worried about me and it changed things. Maybe this, too, was part of that domino effect. Maybe I'd started it after all, and if I did, then I was going all the way with it. There was nothing left to lose.

# CHAPTER 33

I'd never been to this part of the valley before because they tell you it's one place you don't go alone; it's too dangerous. The houses were smaller, there were rusted cars by the curbs, and the kind of people you didn't wanna mess with hanging out in the streets, all Mexican. As I went over the plan in my head, little kids eyed me up and down and ran ahead to tell others. It reminded me of one of my favorite Saturday morning shows, "Ramar Of The Jungle." Whenever Ramar, the great medicine man, would enter forbidden territory, jungle drums would signal that an intruder was approaching. Sure enough, after another half a block, one of the car doors opened and Manuello climbed out as if he expecting me.

"Whatchu doing here, man? Go home if you know what's good for you,"

"I wanna speak to Alfredo."

"He don't talk to chicken-shits."

"If I was chicken, would I be here?" I challenged, hoping I didn't come off too cocky.

Alfredo stepped out of the same car followed by a few of his friends, not that he needed back-up for me. "If you came here to whine about Mounce, forget it. If you came to complain about Eddie, we don't give a shit. It's your fault for taking that skateboard . . . Georgie steals your little girlfriend, they kick your ass all over school, and what do you do?"

Manuello finished the sentence for him, "You bend over and say please sir, can I have another?"

Alfredo took out a cigarette and lit up. "I told you what's what a long time ago. Go home, Canada. You're not gonna make it here."

Manuello stepped up into my face. "Go home, chicken-shit. Maybe your mama'll make you some chicken-shit soup." It was a funny line and everybody laughed. Another time I might have, too, but I figured I'd better say what I came to say even if I was gonna' get my ass kicked for saying it.

"A couple of years ago, a girl got raped. Everybody says it was you, Alfredo." The laughter suddenly stopped. If I didn't make my point quickly I'd be a dead man. "I know it was Georgie."

"You don't know shit, and why're you even tellin' me?

Why should you care?" Alfredo shrugged.

This was the part I'd been practicing in my head since I hatched my plan . . . "I know because Mounce told me, because his father is a lawyer and knew about the case all along. What if I could make the truth come out so that everybody knows you had nothing to do with it, that you were framed? The reputation of a guy like you has gotta mean a lot, right?"

"Alfredo has a 'rep' already," Manuello piped up. "Nobody messes with Alfredo. He's got the respect of everyone in this neighborhood and in a minute you're gonna be on your knees to him!" I tried to ignore Manuello and concentrate on Alfredo, who looked like he was floating the idea around in his head.

"Shut up, Manuello," ordered Alfredo, and then turned to me.

"Why would I care? Nothing'd happen. Nothing'd be different."

"Maybe not now, maybe not today, but what about after you finish school, when you go to get a job, get married, have kids? It's the domino effect, right? What happens now affects . . ." As soon as it came out of my mouth I knew I'd overplayed it. I wasn't his teacher. I only had one trick left in my bag.

"You guys know a couple of weeks ago I got swats

from Mr. Cole. So have most of you. What if I could make him stop–legal like? No more swats for anyone."

"You wouldn't be here unless you wanted something for yourself," answered Alfredo. I was either going to fly or die on my next line.

"You're right, I need you to keep Georgie and Eddie off my back for two more weeks, until the end of the term–just long enough to give me time to . . ."

Manuello straight-armed me in the chest. "Pussy!" he spat out. "Fight your own battles. Get the fuck out of here!"

I took the hint and backed off. "I'm gonna' do it anyway, everything I just said. Without you, even. That's a promise!" On my way back home, I swore to myself I'd follow my plan whether Alfredo helped me or not. I just couldn't stand living like this anymore.

Early the next morning, I was in the parking lot by the convenience store, nervous as hell, not about stealing this time, but about making this next phone call from the pay phone.

"Hello, Mr. Mountjoy? This is Steven Goldman. Somebody I know might have some information about what happened to Ricky that night. But if he told, he would need a favor. Maybe we could talk about it after school?"

Georgie and Eddie had been ignoring me lately. I wasn't sure if they were bored or waiting to plan their next attack, but I didn't care anymore. Nothing was going to change my mind now. After school, I made my way over to Mounce's house, more nervous than I'd ever been. Mrs. Mountjoy let me in and we sat in her living room that looked like a picture out of one of those fashion magazines–everything so neat and in its place.

Mrs. Mountjoy asked me if I wanted a drink but I said, no. I wasn't planning on staying long and after I'd said what I came to say, there was a chance they might throw it in my face when they heard what I was about to say. Mister and Missus waited patiently until I was ready.

"So the first thing this person wants to know is whether swats are legal in school."

"This person has been on the receiving end, I take it?" replied Mr. Mountjoy, cracking a smile.

I nodded and he replied that he'd look into it.

"The next thing is, a couple of years ago, a girl got raped after a school dance. My friend wants to know who the real rapist was."

"Can't help him, sorry," he said, matter-of-factly.

"Then I'm sorry, too."

I stood up to leave, but Mrs. Mountjoy stopped me. "Steven, what has all this got to do with my son?"

Mister Mountjoy answered for me. "He's trying to make a deal, am I right? One bit of information for another?"

But Mrs. Mountjoy had no patience for deals. "Steven,

you have to tell us what you know, and you have to tell us right now!" I remained silent. She turned to her husband, pleading. "Brad!"

This time Mr. Mountjoy gave me one of those dead-serious lawyer looks. "Young man, if you are withholding information from a police investigation, the courts are going to deal very harshly with you."

"It's not me, Mister Mountjoy. You know that Ricky was my friend. It's this other kid, and if I say anything without his okay, I'm in bigger trouble than any court could make for me. You don't know these guys."

With a nod, Mr. Mountjoy let me know me that he did know. Then he gave me a look as if to say we were finally getting down to business. "How do we know this boy will tell us the truth?"

"Cause he was there," I replied without a lie.

There was a long silence as Mr. Mountjoy considered, and then he said, "Tell your friend, no promises, but I'll see what I can do." When he walked me to the door, he handed me his business card and told me that if I heard anything that I should call. I was hoping for better than that, but who was I? Just a kid.

# CHAPTER 34

I liked to take the short cut to school through the field like everybody else. It was faster and I was lazy, though when I think about it, I wondered why I was so anxious to get to school when I hated it so much these days. Anyway, it was a well-worn path, which was both good and bad because this time of the year the grass on either side of me was up to my shoulders. I could see the kids in the playground just beyond the trees and if I ran fast, it would only take a couple of seconds to get onto school property, where no one could jump out at me. I needed to learn to trust my gut more because when I got to the trees, two figures rose up out of the grass—Georgie and Eddie. They knew I couldn't get to school without going past them and if I turned around and ran, they'd be on me like a couple of jackals. I was a dead man until . . .

"Hey, Canada, move your ass, or you'll be late for class. You don't want to get another swat from Cole, do ya?" Alfredo and three of his buddies were standing at the school fence watching for any move Georgie and Eddie might try to make against me. I don't know what changed his mind, but I was thankful as hell.

I had outfoxed them for now, but it just meant that they were only going to try harder to get me next time and I didn't have long to wait before Georgie caught me between classes and body-checked me into the wall. But the Mexicans had an eye out and a second later three of them body-checked Georgie even harder. At lunch period, Eddie and Georgie found me at my locker. Eddie forced my hand inside and Georgie threatened to slam the door on it.

"What are you doin' hanging around with those beaners, Jew-boy? You're surf and they're grease, and the two don't mix. An' you better promise to keep your mouth shut or you'll be a dead surf Jew-boy!"

Luckily a teacher turned the corner and the boys laid off. Georgie didn't slam the locker door on my hand but he did manage to scrape a pencil along my arm leaving a nice welt before he and Eddie walked away. I knew these guys had done some bad stuff in the past, but they must have believed they were in one shitload of trouble to go this far.

Until now, most of the bullying had been targeted at

me. But all that changed when I woke up the next morning to the sound of my father cursing out on our driveway. I opened my drapes to find reams of toilet paper hanging off our trees. He asked me if I knew who did this. I just shrugged, but who was I kidding?

Later I overheard my mom arguing with my dad in the bedroom. "Whatever is going on with Steven and his friends, you have to do something about it!"

"I am not going to fight his battles for him," he argued. "That's not how you learn to take care of yourself."

"Then what should he do, run away from his troubles like you did?"

The next day, Georgie and Eddie completely ignored me at school. Maybe they'd done enough damage and were waiting to see what I'd do next. But when I got home at the end of the day, I learned why: Mom told me that Dad went to speak to Georgie's mother. Outwardly, I was hurt and insulted that he went behind my back when, clearly, I should have taken care of this on my own, like a man. Secretly, I was hoping to God that he threatened to shave Mrs. Sparks head if she didn't make Georgie leave me alone.

When my father got home that night I played it cool; I didn't want to show that it was any big deal. But when he sat me down and told me about his conversation I couldn't believe my ears. Mrs. Sparks said that if anything, I was bullying *her* son and that I should leave *him* alone! For his part Dad promised I would not make contact with her son again. For my part I felt like not only shearing her head, but finishing her off with a baseball bat.

Two days went by and all was quiet. Dad figured his talk had settled the matter and to celebrate informed us that he was taking us all on a trip to the San Diego Zoo. Maybe he thought we needed a break, or more importantly, that my mother needed one. Between the attacks on me, the added stress of planning my Bar Mitzvah a second time, and still grieving over her own mother, the weight of it all was taking its toll. She was popping her pills now with every meal. I think in the back of his mind, Dad also hoped that if we went away for a few days, we could return and start over with a clean slate. Anyway, he packed all six of us into the car and off we went. It actually ended up being a great trip and he was right. It wasn't that we hadn't seen lions and monkeys and elephants before, but it gave us a couple of days to relax and enjoy being with each other—no fighting, no arguing. Even Mom laughed like a kid again.

By the time we got back to L.A., it was night and traffic was snarled because of a road block up ahead. Sitting on a bridge above us were two army trucks with soldiers standing on the overpass. We drove up to what looked like a check point and my father rolled down his window to ask the National

Guardsman, "What's going on?"

"Watts, up ahead. Just follow the car in front of you, sir, you'll be alright," he replied. Now, we'd seen rioting before on T.V., but these were real soldiers with real guns, and down the block just out of sight there were real people in the streets burning and looting.

"Has the whole world gone mad?" my mother muttered. Maybe. Maybe it was an omen, maybe that stupid end-of-the-world fantasy I had had while sitting under my desk a year ago was about to come true.

It was late when we finally pulled into our driveway. The neighborhood was as quiet as a tomb, which was appropriate since we were all dead tired. Mom and Dad climbed out of the car, carrying the two little ones. My father unlocked the front door to realize there was no such thing as a clean slate. The walls of our home had been kicked in and our furniture was overturned and broken. And there was something else; spray-painted on the walls were the words "Kikes go home." My parents told us to stay where we were but Paul and I charged around the house to find more disasters. When we got to our bedroom we found all our clothing pulled out of the drawers. My tallis lay on the floor, ripped to shreds. I looked in the corner of the room where I kept my guitar and microphone–both gone. Down the hall, I could hear my mother crying, asking why anyone would do such a thing. My father came into the bedroom holding Dustin, who had just woken up to the nightmare.

"Don't touch anything, I'm calling the police."

Half an hour later, two of them showed up.

"It looks like they wanted to do damage more than anything else," said one cop.

"They did more than that. They stole my guitar and mike," I added.

. . . Which was a big mistake because after the second cop asked me to describe all the things I lost he asked, "Do your friends know you own a guitar? Do you know who could have done this? Think. It might have been someone you had a fight with or someone trying to get back at you?"

I shrugged–my second mistake–because by not saying anything, it gave him the go-ahead to keep questioning me. "I know you don't want to get your friends in trouble, but whoever did this is not your friend, understand?"

The other one had been watching me, sizing me up. "Are you afraid that if you tell us who they are, they'll make more trouble? The only way we can stop them, son, is if you tell us who they are."

I knew he was right, and what's more, they made sense. What didn't make sense was why Georgie and Eddie would do something so stupid that would bring in the cops. Were they *trying* to get caught? Because if the cops got them for this, it wouldn't take a Sherlock Holmes to connect us all to Mounce's death. I wanted to give the police their names and have them arrested to save my family any more grief, but if I ratted out Georgie and Eddie, for sure I'd have to answer for my involvement the night Mounce died. Maybe this was what they were counting on, hoping to terrorize me and my family until we moved away and were not a threat to them anymore. This was where I could show those punks they were wrong. This was where I could stand up and do the right thing even if it meant I would get in the worst trouble of my life.

"Sorry, Officer, I can't say."

The first cop suggested that I take another look around for anything else that might be missing from my room while they had a talk with my father, but that was just to get rid of me. I left, then doubled back to listen to my father tell them, "I told you who they are, they've been bullying my son for over a month. I even spoke to one of the kid's mothers."

That's when the second cop made the suggestion, "We know who they are, too, and this is not the first time they've been in trouble. I don't blame your boy for not giving them up. These kids are troublemakers of the first order and they're going to give us more grief as they get older, but there's not much we can do unless we catch them in the act. Off the record, the best advice I can give you is to buy a gun. Next time they come through that door—well, you'll be doing us all a favor."

Shoot Georgie and Eddie? To ask my father, the mild-mannered butcher, to buy a gun, stand in the dark and wait for these punks to break in again and then shoot them dead . . . we were indeed a long, long way from home.

# CHAPTER 35

The next day in class, Georgie was sitting in his seat, smirking as he mimed playing a guitar. Was he actually asking to be shot and killed or did he think he was too smart for everyone? After school, I raced to the nearest plaza and made a call to Mr. Mountjoy, who was in a meeting, so I left the message with his secretary. "Tell Mr. Mountjoy it's Steven Goldman. He promised me some information and I gotta have it right away." Those dominos were crashing down right on top of our house and I had to do something about it.

I stayed in that night, thinking about how everything I was so hopeful about had begun to fade. I had no guitar or microphone, and the dreams I came here with had all turned into nightmares. Dad knocked and entered my room. "C'mon," he said.

"Where?"

"I thought we'd go somewhere, just the two of us."

We got in the car and drove, and when I say drove, I mean way out of the suburbs, into the foothills. He wouldn't tell me where we're going, but we were sure as hell not going for ice cream. I began to wonder if I'd been so much trouble that he was just going to stop the car somewhere in the desert and abandon me there. We kept driving until we passed a sign that read, "Chatsworth Park," and pulled up alongside a couple of dozen cars and trucks. It looked like lightning coming over the next hill.

"What is that, gunfire?" I asked, flushed with fear.

My father told me to get out of the car. Oh, my God, I was right, except he's not going to leave me in the desert; he's going to have me shot–not that I don't deserve it. Like a condemned man, I walked up to the crest of the hill but when I stared down into the gulley I couldn't believe my eyes. It was an army unit, vehicles, soldiers, everything. I got it, he brought me here to enlist! He was going to tell the family that I ran away to join the army and then all of their troubles would be over. But that wasn't it either, because off to the side, I saw a bunch of cameras and crew members.

"It's 'Combat,'–the T.V. series," explained Dad. "One of my customers is in the crew. I thought you'd like to watch them film."

Cool. I was not going to die or even get drafted—yet.

We sat on a couple of boulders and I scanned the area for stars like Vic Morrow, but it was too dark to make out any faces. After a minute my Dad asked, "So, Steven, what's going on with these friends of yours?"

"They're not my friends," I shot back.

"Well, they were once. Then all of a sudden . . . I mean, I thought things were going so well, I thought you were adjusting."

I don't know what made me do it but I turned on him with all the anger that had been growing inside me for the past few months. "That's right, I was wearing the right clothes, combing my hair the right way. I learned how to smoke, how to steal, how to sneak out of the house at night and . . ."

"Wait a minute . . . what?" he said, staring at me like I was a stranger. "Look, I suspected you might be smoking out in the back—you weren't too good at hiding that, but stealing and running around the neighborhood in the middle of the night like some hood? Why would you do that?"

"Because that's what you have to do to fit in here. I'm *adjusting*, Dad, just like you told me to! Oh, and all that crap about not worrying about bullies because 'when you stand up to them they back down' is bullshit! These guys aren't scared of nothing,"

"Then you should've come to me," he replied meekly.

"I did! Jesus, don't you remember when I got in trouble with the skateboard, when they started beating me up every day at school? And what did you do about it?"

"Part of becoming a man is knowing when not to fight, and taking care of problems on your own." he offered, but there was no conviction in his voice, it was like he was reciting something from one of his stupid pamphlets.

I, on the other hand, was just starting to feel the depths of my rage. "Oh yeah? You wanna know what you gotta do to be a man here? Georgie took on his father!" With the guns blazing below and the anger welling up inside me like a volcano, I stood up with my fists clenched. "C'mon! C'mon! Are you chicken?" I shouted at him.

He looked at me for a long time and then he slowly stood up. He was big enough to kick the crap out of me but I was ready. Instead, he put his hand on my shoulder and I realized I didn't have what it would take to go through with it. Maybe I wasn't a man, maybe I'd never be, but he squeezed my shoulder gently, affectionately, and we walked back over the hill, away from "Combat."

Back home, as I brushed my teeth and got ready for bed, I could hear my folks talking across the hall. "It's like I don't even know my own kid,"

Then I heard my Mom say something that floored me: "And what does he know about *you* besides your sayings, your slogans? You want him to grow up, but you don't show him how. You throw him a manual and expect him to come out of his room a man? He needs more than that. When you told him that you never had a Bar Mitzvah, did he think less of you? Didn't you see the love in his eyes when you told him the truth? I'm not saying I know more than you about this, but if you ask me, what he needs most right now is to know that if he's made a mistake, it's not the end of the world. And in a place like this among such people, he needs to feel safe–whatever that takes."

The next day was Saturday and I had made a promise to myself. Waking up before anybody else, I went into the garage to get an axe. The mornings were always warm and it didn't take long to build up a sweat. The bamboo thicket in the backyard was big and the roots were thick, but I was determined to cut it down. I walked up to the stalks and stared at those twelve foot high monsters. Like those young boys in Africa who were sent into the bush, like the Indians of the American West who were sent into the desert, I was here to hack these wild bamboo stalks down, hoping that when I was done, the magic would be bestowed on me and I could return to my house as a man.

After an hour or, so the blisters and the sweat had built up enough that I needed to stop for a break. That's when I saw Vicki watching me from over her fence. She and I had shared a lot of secrets back in that bamboo. Cutting down the thicket felt suddenly like I was cutting down a part of our friendship. Maybe she understood, maybe she didn't, but I still had to do it. A little later, dad came out with a shovel and both of us worked together in silence.

As the sun burned and the sweat mixed with the dirt on our faces and shoulders, I could see there was something more on his mind than just the other night .

"I got into the butcher business, you know, because my father was a butcher before me. When I was a kid, I wanted to stay in school and get an education, but times were tough and the family needed money so I quit school to help out at my father's shop. I must have been fourteen or fifteen. Sometimes my father would take me along on his deliveries. I remember going out with him one day to deliver some meat to one of the shops. The owner greeted us, we kibbitzed a little, and then he went into the back room to get his cash. That's when my father told me to take one of the parcels back to the car. When I asked why, he gave me a look as if to say, 'just do it,' so I did. When I looked back, I saw him take the money for the *whole order*. After that he and I drove away and nothing was said about it again. Steven, when you had that trouble with the skateboard, it brought up some bad memories for me. I was angry at you but I was really angry at my father . . . and myself. My dad was a thief, he made me a thief, and I was afraid . . . it's not the kind of thing a father wants to pass on to his son, understand?"

Just then Mom came out with two glasses of lemonade. "Good work, you two. That's enough for today," she said as she looked over the changes in both the yard and in us. Then she gave me some change from her pocket. "Why don't you go to the store? And ask your brother if he'd like to go with you."

That was a surprising request, mostly because the last time my brother and I went to the store together, I nearly got him killed, which was why I never wanted him with me.

It happened over a year ago. After dinner most nights, I loved to walk to the corner store by myself. It made me feel like a big guy. But as soon as I told my parents I was going, Paul would find out, and demand to come too. All he wanted to do in those days was tag along, and all I wanted was to be left alone, so we played a game that went something like this: I'd head up the street and catch him following me and yell at him to go home. Of course, he'd ignore me and continue until I turned around, and then he'd wait to see what I'd do. If I charged at him, he'd run back down the street and wait until I started back up the road. Then he'd continue to follow me. But this time I was determined to lose him, so when got to the main street I scooted across just as the lights changed, knowing that he'd never go against them. Big mistake. The next thing I heard were screeching tires and a blast from a car horn. I turned around to see a car stopped in the street where my brother was just a second ago. The car horn kept blaring and attracting everyone in the neighborhood. Finally the driver got out and ran over to the passenger side, where Paul was standing frightened stiff as a board, the top of his crew-cut just sticking out over the roof of the car. After my heart kicked in again, I ran back across the street while the demented driver screamed such bloody murder that you'd have thought we'd run *him* over.

"What the hell were you doing, kid?" the driver had demanded, frantic with fear that he'd almost run over a child. "Didn't you see the light was red? Don't you know you never cross against a red light? What's wrong with you?"

Paul was so frightened that he couldn't move a muscle until he saw me and when he did, he latched on to me like he'd never let go. By that time, people had gathered around and the police had shown up. An officer listened to the driver's story and then our story and after things settled down he said he'd drive us home.

All I could think of was what my folks were going do to me when we drove back in a cop car and they found out that I had abandoned my brother, and that he almost got run over. I told Paul that he should drive home with the officer by himself (I needed more time to dream up an excuse), but when the cop tried to put Paul into the cruiser, he clung to me so tightly that he tore some of the skin right off my neck. I had no choice but to drive back with him and face the music, and it was not a pretty tune.

Since then my folks hadn't let me take him anywhere, so letting me take my brother to the store now was Mom's way of telling me that she thought I was mature enough. This time we walked together, side-by-side, no chasing, no tag-along.

The plaza had always been a hang-out for kids who had nowhere else to go on weekends, so it was no surprise to find Georgie and Eddie there with some of the other surfers.

"Hey, kikes. Where ya goin', kikes?" Georgie shouted. Paul and I did our best to ignore them.

There was Blakely and Turner and all the kids who used to be my friends. I wondered if they had ever really been my friends or just on loan from Georgie. When we tried to get past them, they blocked our way and it looked like we were going to take a beating right then and there until someone stepped in.

"I think it's time you boys go out and play in the sunshine," suggested Norm, the store manager, to Georgie and his buddies.

"We give this store a lot of business, ya know," cracked Eddie.

Norm smiled and I could see he was almost hoping

that Eddie and Georgie were going to start up. He lifted one of his short sleeves to show off a blue and purple tattoo.

"Ya know what that is, kid?"

Georgie took a good long, hard look, "U.S. Army."

"That's right, served a full tour in 'Nam. You think you're a tough guy? Wait 'till you meet Charlie over there, buttercup."

I think that if Georgie would have given him the nod, Eddie would have taken on the dude, he was so crazy. But this store is a major hang-out and even if they won, they'd lose because Norm wouldn't let them back in again. Besides, in a fight like that, somebody was bound to end up in the hospital.

Georgie turned and they all sauntered out to the parking lot, leaving my brother and me alone for the moment. The tension eased until I started to wonder if Norm recognized me from the first time I came in with Georgie and Eddie, and then I worried if he knew I stole those candy bars from him a while back. It didn't look like he had a problem with me, so Paul and I bought our treats.

As we readied to leave, I looked into the parking lot and realized we were in for even more trouble: Georgie and the surfers were waiting for us, only now there were more of them, maybe ten. The last time I went to the store with my brother I nearly got him run over. This time I could get him lynched. Norm followed my gaze and shook his head.

"I don't like cops, never did. Don't want 'em around here. And I don't like a fight that's not fair neither. Here kid, call your folks."

He handed me the phone. As if I didn't feel guilty enough for having robbed him last week, he had to save my ass and make me feel even worse. Why was it that whenever I did something wrong, I felt like crap? A guy should be able to do something bad once in a while and not always feel shitty about it, shouldn't he? Georgie and Eddie got away with all kinds of shit and they weren't sorry about anything.

A few minutes later my father drove up. When we got into the car, he told me I had done the right thing and for a second I felt better . . . until we drove past Georgie and his crowd.

"Nice car. What model Jew-mobile is that?" I heard as we drove by.

Back at home, there was another high level talk in the bedroom as my father filled my anxious mother in on the details. Finally, they came out and sat us all down in the kitchen: Dustin, Honey, Paul, and me. Mom washed down another pill with a glass of water while Dad laid it on the line for us.

"We had a serious talk, your mother and I. We know how unhappy you are, and we know we can't watch you all the time to make sure you're safe . . ."

"We don't blame you . . ." she interrupted, ". . . and we don't expect you to fight all those boys yourself, it's not fair and it's not right."

My baby sister started to cry as if she understood the seriousness of it all. Even Dustin sensed the tension, so Dad invited him on his lap while he continued. "With all that's been going on, we have two options: we can either move to another area of town or go back to Canada. The choice is yours."

*Mine? I* had to decide the fate of this whole family? I knew it was me that brought on this trouble, that it was my friends who caused it, but why was this suddenly all up to me? It wasn't fair! I didn't want to be responsible for shattering my father's dream and making him go home. And then I got it: he had already made up his mind. He knew we wanted to go back so what he was doing was giving us permission to say it. I couldn't face my troubles, but he was willing to face his. Maybe that's what a man does.

I told my folks that we should wait and see, maybe things would change, even though I knew they wouldn't. But I had been working out a plan and I needed a little more time to see it through. Except I couldn't do it all myself.

# CHAPTER 36

When I told Vicki about my plan the first thing she said was that Mounce's father was stalling and we needed to get him in gear. I called up Mr. Mountjoy and told him I was coming over–it was now or never. Amazingly, he said okay. Jesus, Vicki was good. On the way over, I filled her in on how I was going to use the information he gave me. She pointed out some problems and gave me some more ideas until together, we'd come up with an even better plan.

"This is all I'm prepared to do, Steven," said Mister Mountjoy as he handed me several documents. "Now you have to ask your friend if he's mature enough to do the right thing and tell the truth."

I promised him I would.

At twelve midnight, I sneaked out of my house again,

only this time it was to meet Vicki. We raced down the block, laughing like two teenage spies, all the way to Georgie's house. We sneaked in between the tangled shrubs and worked our way over to his bedroom window to peek inside. There he was, asleep in his bed. Now would be the perfect time to charge in with a shovel and beat him black and blue, but that wasn't the plan. I mean if we did, what would be the fun in that? Kids make all these elaborate plans so they can savor the moment, each step, and there were a lot of steps to our plan. For now, our job was to look around Georgie's room, which was filled with sports equipment, toys, and gadgets. Looking, looking, looking, and there it was–lying on his shelf right out in the open,–my microphone. That's all the proof we needed, off we went, back home.

    The next day Vicki and I went to a surf shop where they sold skateboards. She offered to loan me some money and we bought a real bitchin' one with a picture of a Tasmanian Devil on it, but that wasn't really why I chose that board. It was laminated three times, made of oak wood, and had ball-bearing wheels; the best you could buy. This was for Mounce as much as it was for me.

    Next on the agenda, I caught Alfredo at his locker and got him to sell me a cherry bomb. He didn't want to until I told him what I needed it for. After that, he agreed and I put both the board and the bomb in my locker and waited for the last day of the term.

On that day, the class was rowdier than ever, and while you'd think Mrs. Clarke would be at the end of her rope, there she was standing in front of the class, smiling as happy as a clam (not that I'd ever seen a smiling clam).

"I'd just like to say, it's been a pleasure teaching you this term," she began. Which was a weird thing to say, considering how the term had gone.

Georgie and Eddie looked my way with a mixture of murder and glee in their eyes. "Field, after school," they mouthed.

But I shook my head no and mouthed instead, "Dance in gym."

"Students." Mrs. Clarke waited to catch all our attention and then continued, "I'm going to let you all in on a little secret. I'm retiring."

The class broke into cheers as if this had been their year-long project and they'd just gotten an A. Mrs. Clarke waited patiently for the snickering to die down and then went on in her cheery voice.

"I wanted to leave you with a token of my appreciation for your efforts. One third of the class will be repeating your grade next year."

The room went silent for the first time.

"Now I know you are all anxious to know which of

you will be affected, but I really can't be bothered to tell you, so I've asked Mr. Cole to call each of your parents and give them the news personally. Have a nice summer."

With that Mrs. Clarke closed her books, left the room, and the chaos erupted.

"The bitch!"

"She can't do that!"

"My folks'll kill me!"

I always thought Mrs. Clarke was smarter than the kids gave her credit for, and this proved it. If this was *her* year-end test, I had to give her full marks. I walked out and headed straight for my locker; it was time to set the second part of my own 'test' in motion.

Eddie, whose locker was not far from mine, came lurching around the corner, mumbling, "My father could buy this fucking school!"

I smiled my most sincere smile. "Hey, Eddie. I don't wanna fight no more. Let's make a deal." I reached into my locker for the skateboard, the one I'd taped the cherry bomb to underneath. I lit the wick with the lighter Alfredo gave me, put the board on the floor, and kicked it down the hall to him. The noise of the wheels on concrete masked the sound of the burning wick.

"Not too shabby," he said.

"Oak wood, laminated three times, ball-bearing

wheels. Give it a try."

Alfredo was watching from down the hallway as Eddie climbed onboard and sailed toward him with that stupid grin of his . . . until the explosion lifted him three feet into the air and sent his ass into some potted thorn bushes. A minute later, every student and teacher in the vicinity came running, including Mr. Cole.

"Eddie Lopez, I don't care who your father is, I won't stand for this kind of horse play! Get up and march to my office, pronto!"

*Grab your ankles, Eddie.*

Alfredo gave me a thumbs up and I signalled him to meet me at the school gym next.

As I expected, every student in the school was lined up at the gym doors for the last big dance of the year. I watched from a distance as Georgie's friends broke the news to him.

"Hear about Eddie? Last day of school and he gets caught for lighting a cherry bomb in the corridor. Cole's got him in his office right now!" Georgie shook his head while the crowd started their game of push and shove. This time, however, Mr. Hunter, the gym teacher, was onto them, and nobody got in free–unfortunately, I couldn't take credit for that. I was off to the back of the stage to find my friend, Mike, one of The Skaggs.

"It's for Mounce," I pleaded. "You know his dream

was to play at the school dance. Just one song?"

Mike gave me the okay, and I headed into the wings, where I'd hidden a cardboard box earlier–the next part of the plan. My heart was pounding like a race horse and I wasn't sure if it was because I was actually going to sing in front of the school or because of what Vicki and I had cooked up next.

The Skaggs opened with their first song, dressed as usual in their white pants and surf shirts. I was still waiting in the wings imagining how it would have felt if that was Mounce and Ronnie and I playing in front of everyone. When they finished, Mike made the announcement over the loudspeakers.

"Uh, seeing as this is the last dance and all, we got somethin' special for you today."

He nodded to me and I took a big gulp as I walked out onto the stage holding the microphone. "Hi. Mounce, Ronnie and I had a band called The Vulcans, and we wanted to play at this dance. Well, you all know about Mounce, so this is for him." Mike handed me his guitar and we played a Beatles tune together. It was a little rough, because there'd been no time to practice, but everybody knew it and it sounded pretty good. "If I fell in love with you / Would you promise to be true / And help me understand? / Cause I've been in love before / And I found that love is more / Than just holding hands . . ."

Some of the kids watched while others started to slow-dance. Even Mr. Cole smiled for the first time I could remember as he listened by the door. I was hoping my heart would have settled down by now, but it was beating as hard as ever, probably because it knew what was coming next. When I finished the song some of the kids shouted for more.

"Actually I do have one more."

Mike gave me a look as if I'd crossed the line. Another song was not part of the plan. Instead I took out the piece of paper from my back pocket, the one Mr. Mountjoy gave me.

"This is not the words to a song, it's a legal document from Mounce's dad, who's a lawyer. It's about corporal punishment–swats."

Mr. Cole's smile vanished and he pushed his way through the crowd to try to cut me off, but Alfredo and his gang formed a line in the front of the stage. The V. P. hesitated. I knew I only had a couple of minutes so I read loud and clear.

"It says corporal punishment is legal but only with the permission of the parents. Mister Cole, my parents never gave you permission to use your paddle on me."

Red in the face, Mr. Cole forced his way through the Mexican line and stomped onstage. With one hand, he grabbed the paper and with the other, he clutched the back of my neck.

"Come with me right this minute!" he growled.

His grip felt like a steel vice but as he tried to escort me down the stairs, I wriggled free and ran to the side of the stage. He thought I was trying to get away, but instead I surprised him by returning to the stage with the cardboard box I had hidden earlier. Then I shouted to the crowd, "You can all read for yourselves!" and I threw the reams of copies into the audience as the kids went nuts. With all the panic and commotion, Mr. Cole didn't know whether to go after me or the papers. That's when I grabbed the mike and said what I really came here to say.

"Two years ago, a ninth grader, Mary Ellen Middleton, was raped in the field after a school dance just like this one. They say a Mexican did it."

The audience went silent and every person in the gym turned accusing eyes to Alfredo, who was still standing at the foot of the stage. I pulled out a second sheet of paper from my back pocket and held it up.

"This is also from Mounce's dad, who worked on the case. It wasn't Alfredo, was it, Georgie? It wasn't a Mexican, was it, Georgie? Who was it, Georgie?"

Georgie's face turned white as if Mounce walked right up to him and kicked him in the balls, then he bolted out of the gym. This set off a clatter so loud that the gym sounded like a prison yard about to explode. Surfers and greasers started calling each other out to fight. Whistles went off and teachers surged in like guards ready to put down a riot. Then somebody pulled a fire alarm and everybody ran for the doors. Mr. Cole grabbed me again by the scruff of the neck, but this time I didn't bother to fight back. I had done what I came to do.

"Let's see what your parents have to say about how you've disgraced yourself here today."

Through clenched teeth I answered, "They're waiting for your call, sir." Sure, it was a lie, but it was worth it just to see his reaction.

An hour later, my mother showed up, listened respectfully to what Mr. Cole had to say about what happened, and then politely answered, "Thank you, but after seeing how you've run this school, I've decided this place is not good enough for my son. We'll be making other arrangements for next year. Goodbye."

We left the office and walked out the front door past the honor student—the same one who was there the day I entered Christopher Columbus Junior High. On the way home, I confessed to everything I did and though I expected some yelling, there was none.

# Today I am a Man

# CHAPTER 37

"You bluffed him?"

Vicki and I were sitting side by side on her bed. She stared at a blank sheet of paper while I was staring at the mounds of underwear laying on her floor. This was the second girl's bedroom I'd been in, and unlike Tracy's, which was all prim and proper, this one was a lot more interesting. I could hear Vicki talking, but all I could think about was this urge to roll around in that pile of undies like a puppy dog in a snow bank. Then I noticed Agent 007 staring down at me from a poster on Vicki's wall and I thought maybe that wouldn't be so cool.

"You bluffed him?" she asked again with a look of amazement in her eyes.

"Mr. Mountjoy wouldn't give me any proof that it was Georgie who attacked the girl so I had to do something."

She stared at me like I was some kind of super agent and then kissed me on the cheek.

"Well I guess there's only one thing left to do," she said. Vicki picked up the phone and used her sexiest actress voice. "Hello, Georgie? Hi, it's Vicki. I heard about what happened at school today and I can't believe it . . . I feel so bad . . . do you want to come over tonight? Late?"

Vicki got the answer she expected and signed off with, "Sounds good to me, too."

She put down the phone and smiled at me, but in a different way this time. What we were planning was sneaky and wrong but exciting as hell. Even more exciting was when she flipped open her paperback and read. *"Bond's hand was on her left breast. Its peak was hard with passion. Her stomach pressed against his."*

Vicki stopped reading and looked deep into my eyes. "I don't go all the way,"

"Neither do I."

Vicki dropped the book on the bed and moved in to kiss me, asking me to close my eyes this time. Our first kiss. Funny that when you close your eyes a whole new world opens up. First came this tingling feeling that started here and went all the way down there. Then other sensations came alive—the smell of the girl and the taste of her, like candy—well not the taste of candy so much as the hunger that makes you want more. Weird, but for some reason the memory of the first time I had snuck out of the house late at night came back to me. It felt strange, wrong, and good, all at the same time. My mind drifted to, of all things, singing, and it was as if one of life's secrets was revealed to me in that kiss. I realized that I sang not because I liked to so much, but because I *had to*, like some force deep inside me was trying to burst out and during that kiss my whole body was singing at the top of its lungs, "I wish they all could be California Girls!"

"My beshert," the word escaped me before I knew what I'd said.

"What?"

"Nothing, it means . . . friend."

Our hands were everywhere and even though it was my first time on a bed with a girl, I was pretty sure 007 was looking down at me with approval. After a while, I had to pull away, afraid I was heading over a cliff I wouldn't be able to bring myself back from. Just as well, Vicki and I were going to need all our strength if we were going to succeed in the last part of our plan later on that night.

The clock on the side of my bed finally read eleven-thirty, and I turned to make sure my brother Paul was asleep before pushing two pillows under the covers and rolling out of bed fully dressed. I tip-toed to the bathroom where I dumped my bathrobe under the sink, grabbed my shoes, and slipped out the window, hoping this would be the last time I would have to do this. When I got to the front of my house, Vicki was waiting for me. There was that tingling feeling again! I walked over, took the cigarette from her mouth, gave her a kiss on the lips, and snuffed her cigarette out on the sidewalk. She laughed and we ran down the street to complete our mission.

A few minutes later, we were at Georgie's house and sneaking up to his bedroom like the night before.

"What if Georgie didn't go for it?"

"Are you kidding? she said. "He's probably waiting under my window right now, creaming his jeans, so I wouldn't waste any time if I were you."

God, we made a great team! I took a big breath and straightened up to look through the window. Something was in Georgie's bed, in fact, the same thing that was in my bed–two pillows hidden under the covers. We expected the window would be unlocked so he could let himself back in after he returned from Vicki's house, and we were right. I slid open the window and hoisted myself up into his bedroom, while Vicki waited outside. The first thing I went for was my mike, which was still on the shelf where I saw it last. I wondered what kind of lie he told his mother when she saw that sitting there. I stuffed the mike into my pants and searched for my guitar next. If it was here, it could only be in a few places. I looked under the pile of Georgie's clothes and then in his closet. Nothing.

"C'mon! He'll have figured I'm not showing by now!" Vicki whispered from outside where she was anxiously waiting.

There was nowhere else to hide a guitar except under the bed, and sure enough, when I looked, there it was. I wrestled it out from under and passed the case to Vicki.

"Mission accomplished, 006!" I whispered as I climbed back out the window.

At this point in a Bond movie James usually got a kiss from the girl, his reward for an outstanding job–unless there was a surprise ending. As soon as my feet touched ground I got mine.

"That's called breaking and entering, pal," said Georgie from inside the dark room. "You're in a lotta trouble." Georgie and Eddie were standing there on either side of Vicki, holding her by the arms.

"You're the one in trouble. This mike and that guitar are stolen property. I reported them to the police when you broke into my house and they have a record of it." Bond definitely would have improvised just I was at such a moment.

"Possession is nine tenths of the law," argued Georgie. "A 'course you're welcome to argue that with my lawyer here."

Eddie offered me one of his famous shit-eating grins. "I'd love to talk more, but Vicki and I have a date, right Vicki?" Georgie said, grabbing her by the hair and pulling her down the side of his house toward toward his backyard. "If you keep quiet, maybe I'll let Steve off with a fine and a warning." I heard him cackle.

It was just me and Eddie now, and he'd been itching for me to make a move. "Can't ya just imagine what he's going to do to her?" he asked climbing out the window and standing up to me at his full height.

It was that pissy smile of his that did it. I clenched my fists and ran at him with everything I had, which was exactly what he was expecting because he moved quickly to the side and tripped me, neat onto the grass. I turned back to see him laughing, but I couldn't hear him because a sound like Niagara Falls was roaring in my ears. I got up and ran at him again but again he sidestepped me, this time knocking me sideways with a punch to my head. Down I went, like a drunk fighting a ghost. Vicki cried out from in back of the house and the sound of her panic fueled the rage inside of me. I charged Eddie yet again and this time he dropped me with a searing uppercut, blinding me in an explosion of stars. Then the kicking started and all I could do was protect myself. Ultimately, that's what saved me because he got the surprise of his life when his foot connected with the microphone.

"Ow!" he screamed.

I pulled the mike from my pants and smashed it against his shin bone. Another yelp! I let the overpowering rage within me take over and with my eyes squeezed tight, I furiously pounded him in the same spot again and again until Eddie's yelps turned into cries and he fell to the ground, grabbing his bleeding shin.

I stumbled along the narrow pathway alongside Georgie's house to the backyard where I made out two forms on the grass; Georgie was on top of Vicki, pulling her clothes off while she tried to fight him off. He was so busy with her, he didn't know I was there until I pounded my microphone into his spine. The scene reminded me of the time I saw him pounding on Alfredo. What a great guy I thought he was back then. Georgie turned around, hurt and surprised, and tried to wrestle the mike out of my hand. That gave Vicki the opportunity to knee him in the groin and crawl away.

"You are a dead man!" Georgie sneered. He got to his feet and snapped off a kick to my chest, knocking the breath out of me. Then he grabbed the mike and spoke into it.

"So, hero, got any last words for our studio audience?"

Georgie raised the microphone to slug me, but a hand held him back. "I do."

The three of us turned to find my father standing behind Georgie. In the midst of the fight, nobody had noticed him arrive.

"I'm a minor, you can't touch me," brayed Georgie.

"Touch you? The police told me to shoot you!"

Dad threw a solid punch into Georgie's stomach, but Georgie clipped him on the side of the head with the mike. My father never hit us, even when he was angry, so I've never seen him in a rage. But I saw it then as he slammed Georgie against the side of the house. Georgie bounced off the wall to come back at him but Dad caught him up short and shoved him back again, harder this time. Each time Georgie rebounded off the wall, Dad shoved him back until the fifth or sixth time, Georgie collapsed to the ground, exhausted, blood trickling from the side of his slimy mouth. My father wrenched the microphone from Georgie's hand and said, "That belongs to my son. Let's go, you two."

Dad walked us away, keeping an eye on Georgie who lay whimpering on the ground.

"How'd you know we were here?" I asked, catching my breath.

"You're not as smart as you think. Your brother woke up when you sneaked out of the house and came to tell your mother and me. Didn't take much to figure out where you were going. But don't you say a word to him. Paul told me, not to rat on you, but because he was worried and didn't want you to get into trouble, understand?" I did.

As we walked to the front of the house, Mrs. Sparks came tearing out of her house with Eddie at her side, screaming, "What've you done to my son?"

"Something you should have a long time ago," answered my dad.

TODAY I AM A MAN

# CHAPTER 38

## THE PRESENT

"That sounds suspiciously like a line from a movie," remarked Linda after having listened to the rest of my story.

"It does a little, doesn't it?" I agreed.

"And some of those revenge tactics sounded a little too contrived, as if they were a young boy's fantasies rather than what really happened."

My wife looked me in the eye and asked me straight out. "I have been patient up to this point and listened to everything you had to say, but now I need to know how much of that was true and how much was made up?"

I told her the truth: the events that led up to and after Mounce's death were real. The plans I devised to get my revenge were all fiction. I didn't sing at the last school dance or make a fool out of Mister Cole. Vicki and I never went after Georgie and Eddie, I never retrieved my guitar and microphone, and my father never rescued me. The truth was, after Georgie and Eddie broke into our house, my mother became a nervous wreck so when my Dad gave us the choice of moving to another part of town or going home, we left L.A. for good and returned to Toronto. The Mountjoys never learned the truth about their son.

Linda shook her head incredulously. "Why would you even bother to make up such a story then?"

Because, I thought, this was how a thirteen year old needed to remember it. After all, it was L.A., the land of dreams, Disneyland, Frankie and Annette, where every story had a happy ending.

A million things went through my mind on the day of my actual Bar Mitzvah, things like what presents I was going to get, and how much money I could keep for myself. And constantly lurking below the surface, like a hungry shark, was the fear of screwing up in front of my family and friends. But most of all I wondered how reciting those prayers were going to turn me into a man.

They didn't. Becoming a man for me didn't happen in one magical moment. It happened little by little, after I had the chance to total up all the best and worst moments of my life

—but only after I added them up honestly.

All my life I hoped to grow into the man I promised myself I'd be as a child—a combination of movie heroes, my father, maybe a teacher or two, and all of the qualities I developed along the way. The question that faced me now was, had I grown into *that* man, and if not, what kind of man had I grown into?

What I did know was that I was not about to allow history to repeat itself with my son. I would do for him what my father could not do for me. If that meant being immature, or if it meant holding onto a pain I should have outgrown years ago, then so be it. My wife was right about one thing though: things were different today, and I couldn't beat Todd Holloway the same way I dreamed of meting out justice to Georgie Sparks. Or could I?

## Today I am a Man

# CHAPTER 39

    I kept my promise and did not try to contact Todd or his family in any way after the initial hearing. I kept to myself, went to work and came home, staying in most nights. I avoided my neighbors and when any stopped me to ask how things were, I gave them a quick "fine" and moved on. Daniel had not been bothered for a week. Maybe giving Todd a taste of his own medicine was enough and I looked forward to putting the whole mess behind me. I should have known better.

    We were watching American Idol one night when there was a loud knock at the door. When Linda went to open it, I heard a huge splash of water followed by a loud shriek. I came running to find the vestibule flooded and my wife soaked from her waist down. Someone had filled a large garbage can with water and leaned it up against the front door so that when it was opened, the weight of the can spilled gallons of water.

"Who could have done this?" she screamed.

There was no doubt in my mind. When Todd learned that I would have to go to court to face assault charges against him, he took that to mean that he had won the battle and was now gearing up to win the war. This new tactic was designed to hook me into breaking the court order and coming after him. My wife was right, this was not 1963, and I could not fight that fight. Well, she was half right: it was not 1963, but this was a fight I could win. I just had to be smarter this time.

I took my cue from my children. Whenever they had a problem they needed to solve they came not to me, but to the internet. It didn't take long to find what I needed there: a wonderful little gizmo called a wireless digital night-vision camera. The next day, when everyone in my home went off to school or work, I bought two of these babies and set one up by the front door and a second by the back door. Now whenever someone trespassed on my property, day or night, motion sensors would be tripped and anything within sixty feet would be recorded on my PC. Best of all, whoever approached would not be aware they were being recorded.

I also bought my son a watch off the internet. Not just any watch, but a watch that had a built-in camera and recording device so that if Daniel was picked on anytime or anywhere, there would be a record of it that he could play back on his cell phone.

For the next three days and nights, there was peace and, again, I hoped things had settled down. Then one morning as I left the house to go to work, I found garbage all over my lawn. It wasn't a very clever prank and whoever did it lacked the artistic flair we had had when we were young, but it got my attention nonetheless. After the initial shock of having my private property desecrated, I started to laugh. This time I had him! The good news was that I had recorded three kids tossing garbage all over my lawn. The bad news was that all of the little bastards were dressed in black hoodies. I looked for any distinguishing clothing or tags, but it was like watching shadows at play. They were smart enough to keep their mouths shut as well, so that there was not even a voice that could be used to identify them. The frustration of losing another round to these young thugs irked me, but the worst of it was that old feeling of being helpless against a gang of teenagers again, as if I had never gotten away from them. Was life trying to tell me that you can't change history, or change who you are? Again my wife's words returned to me, "You cannot win a fight that happened over thirty years ago!"

# Today I am a Man

# CHAPTER 40

A few nights passed without incident. I knew Todd was hoping I would retaliate, but I wasn't going to take the bait, which meant that if he was going to step up this game, he'd have to come after either Daniel or me next. I didn't have long to wait.

No one noticed a kid wandering through the parking lot that day at work and though I took steps to protect my home and my family, I never thought this punk would take the battle this far afield. My mistake, because when I came out of my office that afternoon, all four of my tires were slashed. I had been bested and humiliated to the point that if I could have put my hands around the kid's neck right then and there, I would have, which, I guess, was exactly what he was going for. He was fifteen and I was fifty, he had youth but I had experience . . . a different tactic was required.

My court date was fast approaching and I was desperate to find proof of Todd's vandalism. Not that that would mitigate my assault offense, but at least I would have something I could wave in front of my family, the kid's parents, the police, and the whole world to show them that I was not the monster I was being made out to be. That's when I realized the trap I had set for myself: this all began as an attempt to protect my son from a bully, but as Linda pointed out, it was becoming *my* fight against the demons of my past. Well if it was, fuck it; I was going to bury those demons once and for all.

Going over the surveillance tapes for the umpteenth time, my mind wandered back to the old days, and the hurt and anger started to well up inside me again. But with that I also remembered that bullies like Todd and Georgie needed a crowd, someone they could perform for and brag to, otherwise it wasn't fun. There were three kids throwing garbage on my lawn that night, which meant that Todd would have had to have contacted his friends to plan the prank.

I returned to my computer and did some more internet research until I came upon a new cutting-edge software program I could download onto my cell phone that would allow me to overhear conversations on other people's cell phones, a kind of wiretapping without wires. For this, Daniel and I had to be co-conspirators because I needed Todd's cell phone number. If this kid and his buddies threatened or attacked him directly, as I suspected they would, I would be one step ahead of them.

I only had four more days before my court date, so I monitored Todd's phone calls whenever I could to see if he was chatting with his buddies about his next caper, but it was a time-demanding, hit-and-miss affair and my marketing business was beginning to suffer. And to give the little prick credit, he pulled no more pranks. Maybe he finally concluded that I wasn't going to come after him.

I told Daniel to forget the whole thing, that I would take my punishment from the courts and live with it. But it was my nature not to give up and I returned again and again to those tapes until one night Daniel came into my study and caught me. We watched together for a while, and then it was Daniel who found the proof we needed: their running shoes. It was true that all the boys wore black clothing and hoodies that night, but they were also wearing running shoes, and shoes being as expensive and unique as they are these days, Daniel was able to identify each one of the kids by them. The second thing Daniel noticed was a car parked on the other side of the street that he knew belonged to one of the boy's parents. This might not be evidence that I could use in a court of law, but in the court of public opinion, well, that was another story.

I reached back into my childhood and seized upon an idea I dreamed up but never had the guts to use against my nemesis, Georgie Sparks. Daniel and I made a copy of the video featuring the three masked boys running around on our lawn, and then added captions beneath it, identifying the running shoes and the car. My idea was to email this to Todd's parents, but my son reminded me about the no contact condition in my bail bond, so we did the next best thing: We posted the video on Daniel's Facebook page and invited all his friends to see it. It didn't take long. Within three hours, we received an irate phone call from Todd's father demanding we take down the video or we would be sued. Now it was time to bring the full force of the past to bear upon the present.

"Mister Holloway," I said calmly, "What you saw on Daniel's Facebook's page was only a sample of what we have on your son and his friends. If you like, I can provide you with the internet address of the store where you can see the night video camera that I used to catch your son *twice*, once when he he set up a pail that doused my wife with water a week and a half ago, and second, when he and his friends tossed garbage on my lawn. You will also see on that website a watch I bought my son which records voices or threats, and the software that allows a person to listen in on the cell phones of others who are busy planning pranks against their neighbors. Now this may not be admissible in court, but don't you think it's time you had a talk with your son?"

Thirty minutes later, there was a knock on our door. I opened it to find Mister Holloway with Todd and the other two confederates, all standing there contritely. Todd spoke first. "Mister Goldman, I am sorry for what I did, the water, the garbage . . ."

"And what else?" prompted his father.

"And I'm very sorry about hitting Daniel that night at the party and all the other stuff."

"And?"

"And it won't happen again, I promise."

I nodded to Todd and said, "You guys were all friends once; I hope you can be friends again. I hope we can *all* be friends, but just so you know, if you hurt my son or anyone in my family again, I will publish the rest of the videos and then I will kick your ass."

My wife who was also at the door was about to reprimand me when Mister Holloway broke in. "You won't have to, because I'll do it myself. Now I don't know about the court case, Mister Goldman. If they won't drop charges, at least I can put a word in with the judge."

"Thank you. I'm prepared for whatever happens," I replied. "Daniel will take the video off of his Facebook page for now. Thanks for coming over."

I put out my hand out for each of them to shake–which they did, and then they left. As I watched them return to their car, my father's words drifted back to me: *You know what you do when a bully comes at you? You stand up to him, because if you don't, he'll keep coming at you again and again. Pass the California melon, please.*

Linda turned to me with satisfaction and a even little admiration. "Now tell me how you got him to do that," she asked.

I showed her the surveillance tapes.

"But you *didn't* have any other proof," she wondered out loud.

"I bluffed them."

She smiled and shook her head, as if to say, "You're a fool for what you did, and I love you for it." It was a look I imagined Vicki giving me, had I carried out my Machiavellian plan against Georgie, but seeing this now from my wife felt even better. Maybe I was fighting a battle that started over thirty years ago, but it felt like something had finally settled in me. Even so, I enrolled all our children in karate class the next week.

THE END

LARRY RODNESS

## Today I am a Man

## About the Author

Larry Rodness was born in Toronto, Canada and lived there until he moved to Los Angeles with his family in the early sixties. Much of the material for his first novel, "Today I Am A Man", comes from the three years he lived there. Larry currently lives in Toronto with his wife Jodi, and their three children, Adam, Jonathan and Erin.

TODAY I AM A MAN

If you enjoyed *Today I am a Man* consider
these other fine Books from
Savant Books and Publications:

*Essay, Essay, Essay* by Yasuo Kobachi
*A Whale's Tale* by Daniel S. Janik
*Tropic of California* by R. Page Kaufman
*The Village Curtain* by Tony Tame
*Dare to Love in Oz* by William Maltese

Scheduled for Release in 2010:
*The Bahrain Conspiracy* by Bentley Gates
*The Mythical Voyage* by Robin Ymer
*The Jumper Chronicles: The Quest for Merlin's Map*
by W. C. Peever

If you are an author or prospective author who would like
to be published
contact Savant Books and Publications at

**http://www.savantbooksandpublications.com**

Made in the USA
Charleston, SC
15 February 2010